The Wicked Truth about Love

about Love

The Tangles of Desire

Suzanne Ross
Illustrated by Susan Drawbaugh

LOVE QUIZ
FREE MUSIC DOWNLOADS

The Wicked Truth About Love: The Tangles of Desire
Copyright ©2009 Suzanne Ross

Illustrated by Susan Drawbaugh

Music:

Never Had To Ask
Published 1994
John Batdorf, BatMac Music, BMI
Michael McLean, Shining Star Music, ASCAP

I Never Wanted
Published 2005
John Batdorf, BatMac Music, BMI
Michael McLean, Shining Star Music, ASCAP

Love: All I Really Know About It
Published, 2008
John Batdorf, BatMac Music, BMI
Michael McLean, Shining Star Music, ASCAP

The Wicked Truth About Love website:
http://www.thewickedtruthaboutlove.com
DOERS Publishing website:
http://www.doerspublishing.com
Book Design by Archer Graphics
ISBN 978-0-9818123-0-4

For my husband Keith

In the sweetest dreams I've ever known
I could barely glimpse a love like you have shown
I'm not sure I'm every gonna see
Why you've given all the love you have to me

(Michael McLean, *Never Had To Ask)*

Contents

Music Download Instructions

Long-time musical partners Michael McLean and John Batdorf have graciously made available tunes that musically illustrate the wicked truth about love. Their offering includes some of their classic songs plus original pieces written just for *The Wicked Truth About Love*. These loving, witty and wise tunes are available for free to readers of *The Wicked Truth About Love: The Tangles of Desire*. Just visit www.thewickedtruthaboutlove.com/music, download the music and enjoy.

The Wicked Truth About Love

Introduction

*I*f you keep getting tripped up on the way to love, then this book is for you – which means it's for everyone. (That's for my publicist.) Let's face it, "The course of true love never did run smooth," as Shakespeare knew over 400 years ago. Why does it seem so hard to get love right? And why is it that no matter how many times we get our hearts ripped out of our chest and handed to us in a barely beating bloodless lump, we keep trying? Maybe we're all masochists, or maybe love is just so wonderful that it's worth the pain. But if you've been getting tangled up and trampled under by love's obstacles, you'll be pleased to know that this book is here to help.

I wouldn't be at all surprised if you were wondering why you should trust anything you read in this book. You've probably read the magazine articles, taken the quizzes, and studied the books by noted psychologists, all to no avail. If that's the case, then I have you right where I want you – fed up with all the self-help mumbo jumbo and plain tired of the search for answers. You've broken up so many times that you could write a how-to book about it. In other words, you are more than ready for the truth about how to find love. What I'm going to tell you is not going to sound like anything you've heard before. It will challenge your assumptions and change what you think you know about love.

I have been working with a group of researchers from psychology, anthropology, sociology, theology, brain physiology and philosophy who are exploring something about how human desire works. These are really smart men and women who write in the nearly indecipherable language of academia. Though I myself am no genius, I am just smart enough to figure out what they are saying, which is what inspired the core insights of this book. The big idea they are working on is called *mimetic theory,* and the father of contemporary research into the theory is Dr. René Girard. His work is so important that in 2005 he was inducted into the French Academy, which consists of 40 members called "immortals." (Past members include people like Louis Pasteur, the reason we "got milk" safely; René Descartes, of "I think therefore I am" fame; and Jules Verne, the guy who invented science fiction with books like *Journey to the Center of the Earth* and *20,000 Leagues Under the Sea.* See why they're called "immortals"?) Anyway, Prof. Girard is an immortal now but he doesn't let it go to his head. He is a very gentle and generous man who embodies a spirit of love with everyone, including non-academics like me whose lives have been transformed by his ideas.

As I said, I am no René Girard, but I do have talent and experience in writing, education and instructional design. What I do is take an idea and design a way to teach it. For schools I wrote curriculum; for business, it was training programs and policy and procedure manuals. I've taught preschoolers how to tie their shoelaces and sales pros how to track inventory using new software. What I do in this book is translate mimetic theory from "academeze" to plain speak, so you don't have to go through what I went through: years of struggling to make sense of some really difficult, but important scholarship.

But I do one more thing, something the scholars don't do. No matter what I'm teaching, I keep one question in mind that I want to be able to answer for my learners: **So what?** In other words, why should you bother to learn whatever it is I am trying to teach you? How will it make a difference in your life? Scholars believe that a really good idea is valuable in and of itself, and I agree with that. But the ultimate value of the idea, the true test of its worth, is whether it matters to how we live, love, and work together.

Introduction

When it comes to mimetic theory and the search for true love, the answer to the "So what?" question is simple and profound. With mimetic theory you'll have the key to getting yourself untangled from the things that trip you up on the way to an authentic, sustainable love. You will be able to identify your tangles and extricate yourself from them before they either ruin your chances with a good prospect or pull you in too deep with the totally wrong person. Once the obstacles are removed, your chances for true love will dramatically improve. I invite you to read this book, take the questionnaire, and learn about love from a radical, new perspective.

If you want to learn more about mimetic theory you can go to the Raven Foundation website, www.ravenfoundation.org. My husband Keith and I began the foundation to spread awareness of mimetic theory. This book is part of that effort. Now's the time when I can put into writing the gratitude I feel every day for the people I work with: Keith Ross, Adam Ericksen, Maura Junius and my daughter, Emily Martensen. They are joyful, enthusiastic, smart human beings who make work feel like a holiday. I'd also like to thank Laurie Ashcraft and her firm, Ashcraft Research, Inc. for their work designing the questionnaire; Susan Drawbaugh for her illustrations; Irene Archer for her cover and interior design work; and Cathy Sweitzer for her skill and wisdom during the editing process. The music for this project was provided by Michael McLean and John Batdorf, two men whose compositions about love reflect their own honesty and compassion. I am honored to have collaborated with them. I am also indebted to my friends and conversation partners on mimetic theory and love, James Alison and Andrew McKenna. In particular, I'd like to thank Mark R. Anspach for sharing his insights into the nature of love as gift. And my greatest thanks are always reserved for René Girard, scholar, mentor, immortal and friend.

Love is a teacher, but a hard one to obtain.
Learning to love is hard and we pay dearly for it.
It takes hard work and a long apprenticeship,
for it is not just for a moment that we must learn to love,
but forever.

Fyodor Dostoevsky, *The Brothers Karamazov*

Chapter One

Finally, Someone is Going to Tell Me What Love Is

First A Mind Dump

When I was a little girl (and forgive me if I don't tell you how long ago that was), I couldn't wait to be a woman. I studied the women I knew, my mother and grandmothers, my little Italian aunts and my sturdy Slovakian ones. Then I made a list of things that they had in common, thinking that these were the things that would make me a woman. Because I was a child, the characteristics on my list weren't very profound. They were mostly outward signs, like being a good cook or using hair spray or shaving your legs. (My husband tells me that shaving also figured big in his race to acquire manhood.) So, in pursuit of my womanhood, one day I locked myself in the bathroom and shaved my legs, but about the only the thing that happened was my mom said I was too young to be shaving and I got itchy skin. I also figured out that the scent I liked on my dad was called menthol, but nothing was different inside, and my parents still treated me like a little girl. I had to agree with them. I was just a little girl with itchy legs.

Maybe, I thought, it's the combination of shaved legs with stockings, so I tried that, and still nothing new inside me that I could point to and say, Aha, this is it. I've arrived at womanhood! Maybe it was shaved legs and stockings with high heels? No, that was definitely not it. Maybe it was having a boyfriend who would someday be your husband? But having a boyfriend was a project

1

in itself, so I made a different list for that one which included things like: shave your legs regularly, don't dress like your aunts, don't listen to Grandma's music, be nice, don't argue, wait on him hand and foot.... You can see how that wasn't going to lead to anything productive. But then one day, many years and failed romances later, I woke up and realized that I was a woman, and it had nothing to do with any of the things I thought it had to do with. I can't tell you exactly when it happened or point to a particular cause, but there I was, a woman who had left little girl concerns and ways of thinking behind, and how it happened was a mystery.

So if you're reading this book and were disciplined enough to begin at the beginning, you're no doubt wondering what these first paragraphs have to do with love. You're probably hoping this chapter is going to live up to its title and that really soon now I'm going to tell you what love is. If only I'd put it in bold and set it apart in its own indented paragraph. That would have been considerate of me. Maybe there's an index that will tell you which page it's on, and you could turn to it now because your sense of discipline, not to mention your patience, is wearing thin. All right, here it is; at least here's where we are going to start.

Do you have a list in your head of the things that will happen when you're in love for real like my list for being a woman, things that are the sure signs that you've found the right one and the search is over? Of course you do. We all do. If you want to know what love really is, first you have to download that list from the recesses of your brain and move it to trash. It is for sure a huge obstacle to true love – trust me on this. I'm going to start the list with some of my things and things my friends and family had on their list, and then I want you to add the ones that are in your head that I haven't got down here.

☒ S/he will know my thoughts so well that I won't have to finish my sentences. (I've tried that one – not one of my better ideas.)

☒ S/he will know exactly what to do when I'm _____. (Fill in the blank with your emotion of choice: angry, sad, depressed, anxious, peeved, petty, moody…)

☒ I will think about him/her constantly, except when I'm _____. (Fill in your favorite activity: listening to my iPod™, out with friends, getting my nails done, drafting players for my fantasy football team…)

☒ S/he will complete me. (Whatever that means.)

☒ S/he will give me exactly what I need. (Again, whatever that means.)

☒ S/he will make me completely happy. (Wow, no pressure there.)

☒ S/he will be _____. (Fill in your requisite physical attribute: tall, short, thin, curvy, built, bald [you're welcome], pleasingly plump [you're welcome]…)

☒ _____

☒ _____

☒ _____

Did you add yours to the list? As you can see from my slightly sarcastic parenthetical remarks, I don't believe in this list at all. It's a lot like my becoming a woman list – it is trying to pin down something that is fairly mysterious by listing some outward signs as if acquiring them will produce the thing you're after. Be sure you've added all the things from the list in your head because here it goes: cursor on the mark, get set, drag to trash.

The Greatest Thing

Before you read any further, I'd like to ask you one thing: Why are you reading this book? The page count isn't of the *War and Peace* variety, but still, reading is an investment of your time and energy, and so I'm wondering what's motivating you to read a book about love. You could be reading a book about how to make a million bucks, look younger, lose 10 pounds, improve your vocabulary, count cards at Black Jack, write a killer resume, cook with tofu – the list of self improvement books is endless. But you have chosen a book about love. Allow me to say that no matter your reason, I believe you have chosen wisely.

The lyrics for the song, *The Second Greatest Thing,* * include the phrase, "Loving her's the greatest thing I've ever done." It was written by my friend, Michael McLean and here's how it goes:

Second Greatest Thing

If I wrote a pop song that topped the charts
And everyone sang it
With all their hearts
And it rocked on for twenty years at #1
I'd say it's the second greatest thing I've ever done.

If I wrote a sermon like the one on the Mount
If I had millions
In my account
If I cured cancer and a Nobel Prize was one
I'd say it's the second greatest thing I've ever done.

The Greatest Thing, continued

Cause I've loved her, I kept my promise
I loved her no matter what
And she'll always be the only one
I am not a perfect husband but my heart was never shut
Loving her's the greatest thing I've ever done

The song claims that "loving her" would be the greatest thing he'd done even if the guy had written a hit song, won a Nobel prize, ended hunger, or written the Sermon on the Mount. My friend Michael is saying that every other achievement in the world comes in second place to the achievement of loving another human being well. He's a dear friend of mine and so I know that he's not just saying that to see if he can write a hit song. He believes it and he lives it. Michael always puts his own needs second to those of his wife, his kids, his friends, his parents, even people he hardly knows. He's a giver because he knows something for absolutely, positively sure: the only thing that matters in your life is the love you share, the relationships you nurture, the people you treasure and the people who treasure you. Getting love right isn't just a hobby or a sideline. It's what a life well lived is all about. So congratulate yourself for knowing that and for devoting yourself to the task. Love isn't always easy, but it's always worth it; and no matter who you are or what you have already accomplished or have yet to accomplish, love is the greatest thing you'll ever do. ❤

*Michael McLean, *The Second Greatest Thing*, 2006.

5

The Mystery of Love

You're ready now for the definition of love you've been waiting for all your life and that you had to do that stupid exercise to get to. I know you're thinking, This better be good, and it is, really. The definition of love is this: Love is a mystery. Don't you love that? No? You think I've bailed, dodged the issue, led you on a wild goose chase for nothing? Most people think that when they first hear it. That's okay, just hang in there because by the end of this chapter (which is only three, maybe four more pages, I'm not sure because I haven't written it yet), you are going to be thrilled with it. (Wow! Now *I'm* feeling the pressure.)

I didn't come up with this definition of love randomly. I asked a lot of people I know who have had long relationships (okay, six people doesn't sound like a lot, but when you consider how hard it is to sustain long relationships, I think it's a pretty good sampling) just what love is, and all six of them shrugged their shoulders and just smiled – not at me, at their partner. Isn't that weird? It's as if love is something that they couldn't put into words, but could only express in a smile exchanged with someone who they've been with a long time. *Really* weird and not something that lends itself easily to being an item on a list. In fact, it's a little bit mysterious, don't you think?

So what I figured was that love was a mystery, but that that was a good thing. Most of us don't like mysteries. Well we do, if it's in a book or movie or a one-hour *Law and Order* episode, and we know that a solution, however lame, will be provided for us at the end. But an *eternal* mystery, something that has no solution? Few of us enjoy that. Few of us want to live like that. We want answers, darn it! (That's my harshest swear word – feel free to fill in your own if it makes you feel better.) We are Americans; we're problem solvers; no unknown is too unknowable for us to figure out. We went to the moon; we split the atom; we invented cheese in a can; we are masters of all we survey, right? So we tackle love with the same energy and determination, and the darn thing refuses to submit to our rational analysis.

But reducing love to a problem that can be solved like, How much methane gas does one cow emit in a day, and does it affect global warming? – well, that takes the mystery out of love, and mystery is what makes love so captivating. I mean, once you've solved a problem, you're done with it, and you move on to the next one. Think about it, we haven't gone back to the moon, have we? Do you really want love to be a problem you solve? Because if it is, you will toss it aside and move on to the next problem just like NASA did and just like you did in algebra class. (If you got as far as algebra – I think I did, but I don't remember much except that I couldn't wait to toss aside all those problems.)

Unprovably Real

Love can't be expressed in a mathematical equation or as a scientific hypothesis. That's because math and science are really good at describing the world we can see, feel, hear, touch, and taste, but we don't encounter love through our senses in the same way. Love *affects* our senses, sure. Our heads spin, we hear bells and see shooting stars when we are in love, but it's hard to prove love exists the way we prove the existence of bacteria in pond scum.

The character, Palmer Joss, in the movie *Contact*[1] tries to make this point with Ellie, Jodie Foster's character. She's a young woman still grieving the death of her father that happened when she was a little girl. She's in charge of this huge field of giant antennas trying to pick up some signal from deep space that would prove the existence of extra-terrestrials, but what she's really looking for is some evidence that her dad isn't gone, that even though he's dead, there might be a way to contact him. (Get

[1] *Contact*, dir. Robert Zemeckis, perfs. Jodie Foster and
Matthew McConaughey, DVD, Warner Bros Pictures, 1997.

it, *Contact*?) She won't admit this to herself, of course. She is a scientist who doesn't believe in anything she can't measure, not life after death, not love, not God.

Enter hunky theologian Palmer Joss, played by Matthew McConaughey, who is a walking billboard for how believing in God gives you cute dimples. Here's a snippet of dialogue in which Palmer tells Ellie that proving God's existence is as futile as trying to prove that love exists:

Palmer Joss: Did you love your father?

Ellie Arroway: What?

Palmer Joss: Your dad. Did you love him?

Ellie Arroway: Yes, very much.

Palmer Joss: Prove it.

The kind of proof Palmer is asking for is the kind of proof Ellie is used to providing: scientific proof. His point is that just because you can't prove something scientifically doesn't mean it doesn't exist. All it means is that the thing has a different reality, exists outside the physical world that science and math are designed to measure. Ellie has an experience at the end of the movie that convinces her that extra-terrestrials do exist; she just can't prove it scientifically. Here's how she explains it to a scientific panel demanding proof of her claim:

Panel member: Doctor Arroway, you come to us with no evidence, no record, no artifacts. Only a story that to put it mildly strains credibility. Over half a trillion dollars was spent, dozens of lives were lost. Are you really going to sit there and tell us we should just take this all... on faith? *(pause, Ellie looks at Palmer)*

Michael Kitz: Please answer the question, doctor.

Ellie Arroway: Is it possible that it didn't happen? Yes. As a scientist, I must concede that, I must volunteer that.

Michael Kitz: Wait a minute, let me get this straight. You admit that you have absolutely no physical evidence to back up your story.

Ellie Arroway: Yes.

Michael Kitz: You admit that you very well may have hallucinated this whole thing.

Ellie Arroway: Yes.

Michael Kitz: You admit that if you were in our position, you would respond with exactly the same degree of incredulity and skepticism!

Ellie Arroway: Yes!

Michael Kitz: (*standing, angrily*) Then why don't you simply withdraw your testimony, and concede that this "journey to the center of the galaxy," in fact, never took place!

Ellie Arroway: Because I can't. I... had an experience... I can't prove it, I can't even explain it, but everything that I know as a human being, everything that I am tells me that it was real! I was given something wonderful, something that changed me forever... A vision... of the universe, that tells us, undeniably, how tiny, and insignificant and how... rare, and precious we all are! A vision that tells us that we belong to something that is greater than ourselves, that we are not, that none of us are alone! I wish... I... could share that... I wish, that everyone, if only for one... moment, could feel... that awe, and humility, and hope. But... That continues to be my wish.

When Ellie says, "I was given something wonderful, something that changed me forever," she could easily be describing what love is. What she discovers is that this experience that she can't prove but can only give witness to is the thing that heals her grief over her father's death and opens her heart so that she can accept the love offered to her by Palmer Joss. Maybe love is one heck of a hallucination that we should be responding to with "incredulity and skepticism," but Ellie can't do that anymore. Because of her unprovable but undeniable experience in space, love has become a mystery that she no longer needs to deny, as she did with the existence of God, but finally can just allow to be and to be mysterious.

Mystery itself may be the thing that pulses through the fabric of the universe giving it its very being. A mathematician named Kurt Gödel astounded his colleagues – one of whom was Albert Einstein – by using mathematics to prove that there are equations that are both true AND unprovable.[2] I wish I'd known about this in high school algebra because every time I couldn't prove an equation I got graded with a big red zero. Gödel proved that being mathematically unprovable is not a disqualifier for truth. Sounds like what Ellie figured out about extra-terrestrials, God and love.

Scientists also think that over 95 percent of the universe is made up of matter and energy that can't be seen or directly measured by any instruments we currently have, only inferred to be there by however scientists infer things about the universe. They call it "dark matter" and "dark energy" because they figure it must be dark or they could see it. That's one great big honking mystery, and maybe someday scientists will figure out what's going on in the "dark," but I'd wager my snapshot of a UFO landing in my backyard that when they unravel that mystery, they'll realize there is some other big mystery out there they never even knew they didn't know about.

[2] Rebecca Goldstein, *Incompleteness: The Proof and Paradox of Kurt Gödel*, (New York and London: 2005).

I Didn't See THAT Coming!

Here's a classic love question: *Do opposites attract?* I always wondered if relationships were stronger the more you have in common or whether differences sustain you over the long haul by keeping things interesting. That question may sound like a good one, but it is a gigantic distraction. Like a slab of red meat tossed to a guard dog, it keeps you from seeing the obvious about all human relationships.

The wicked truth about love is that no matter how alike or different you and your lover might be, you are still two unique people who will never be fully known to one another. Life with another human being will always be full of surprises. In fact, the more alike you are, the more you might be lulled into thinking you are *completely* alike. You'll begin to expect that your beloved will think, feel, react and desire exactly as you do. But another human being is not you, no matter how much you love each other. There's even a mathematical formula that represents this – it has the mysteriously humorous name "asymptote." Take a little trip to Wikipedia (my favorite source for trusted knowledge), and you'll find a graph that looks something like this:

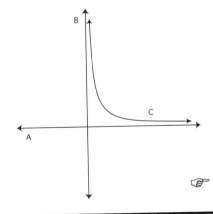

The curved line (C) goes on forever, getting closer and closer to the straight line (A and B), but they never quite touch. Boggles the mind, I know. What we have here is the mathematical formula for infinity (∞) and when you apply it to relationships, you realize that no matter how close you get to someone, you will never really close the gap between you completely.

So when your partner does something that has you smacking your head and muttering, "I didn't see that coming!" you may feel shocked, stupid, embarrassed or afraid that you've made a monumental mistake by getting involved with someone capable of whatever the crazy thing is s/he said or did. In those moments it's important to take a deep breath and realize that the whole shocked and surprised scenario has been artificially created by false expectations. When someone does something "unexpected," what they are doing is being themselves in all their mysterious unknowability. Instead of it triggering some sort of red alert, it is really a signal that something incredibly fascinating and wonderful is suddenly possible – you have been given an opportunity to delve deeper into the mystery of your beloved. Rather than freak out, start listening. Ask questions, wait for the answers, and be prepared for the thrill of discovery. 🍂

The Joy of Not Knowing

I'm pretty sure that no one is ever going to solve the mystery of love. It is an eternal mystery that will never be reduced to an equation or step-by-step analysis. There will never be a "if you do this thing you'll find true love" formula, no matter how many authors, theologians, psychiatrists, Dr. Phils and Dr. Lauras, best friends or moms tell you they have the answer. And there will never be an explanation for why two people are attracted to each other in the first place.

Remember the TV show, *Dharma and Greg*?[3] No formula could have predicted that they would find true love together. In fact, everything we think we know about what makes relationships work says, No way, those two will never make it. Here's how the couple is described on a website about the show:

> There could hardly be an odder match, but love knows no reason. Assistant DA Greg Montgomery, the golden spoon son of successful businessman Edward Montgomery and his bossy spouse Kitty, the queen of socialite snobism, falls madly in love with the utterly unconventional free spirit Dharma Finkelstein, truly the daughter of hippie couple Larry Finkelstein and Abby O'Neil, who never fail to go against whatever even smells like convention.

The hippie and the Ivy League Republican – I suppose opposites do attract, but Dharma and Greg are more like the meeting of matter and anti-matter. The show's writers are exploring the mystery of love, asking what exactly is the secret ingredient that makes relationships work and love endure. Here's one answer from the show:

Dharma: You're gonna be a great dad!

Greg: How do you know? How am I gonna know what to do?

[3] *Dharma and Greg,* ABC, 1997-2002.

Dharma: Oh, you'll watch what I do. You'll totally disapprove and do the complete opposite.

That's just silly, of course. Disapproving of everything your lover does and then doing the opposite is not the secret formula for love. Or is it? It works for Dharma and Greg, but would it work for anyone else? All we can say for sure is that they have found their secret formula for love, and it's up to us to find ours. I'd suggest you keep notes as you conduct your search – you may not find love, but you might be generating some pretty good sitcom material.

There is one tip I can give you at this point before we look at the obstacles to love and reach some grand conclusion at the end of the book. If love is a mystery, then instead of tackling love like a to-do list or an equation to solve, why not develop your sense of mystery? Attune yourself to mystery. Learn to love it the way a dog loves liver snaps. You don't want your back end wagging so hard your feet slip out from under you, but a little waggle in the face of mystery wouldn't be a bad thing. How does one cultivate a love of mystery, you ask? It's simple, really. Here's what I do.

My husband and I have a home in a mountain valley, and in the summertime, I love to sit outside and look at the sky. It's usually chilly, because we live in a desert mountain valley, which means when the sun goes down the temperature drops from 90 to 65 degrees in about thirty minutes. So I put on a sweater, set my lawn chair in the driveway in the fully reclined position, and watch the stars. It's amazing! The Milky Way, our galaxy, is a double band across the sky so dense with stars that it's, well, milky. The air is so thin and the sky so crystal clear that you can actually see satellites moving across the dome of the sky. And every night, I mean *every* night, I see at least one shooting star. No kidding. I see Jupiter and Mars and billions and billions of stars, and it's vast and utterly beautiful. I realize that I am staring into eternity, into something that defies explanation, and I feel happy about it! It's truly amazing, and I am happy just being amazed without having to understand or explain it to myself or anyone else.

So here's your job before you read the next chapter. Find your version of my summer sky. It could be something simple, already right in front of you, like contemplating the beauty of a flower or the flight of a bird. It's probably something in nature, because nature is mysteriously beautiful. Maybe it's autumn, and the leaves are changing color, or it's summer, and there's a dynamite lightning storm over your house, or the snow is falling in winter, and you realize that it's never quieter than when it's snowing. Just contemplate anything that won't let you explain it away, and let the joy fill you up. Because the thing about mystery is, if you let yourself live with it, it leads to joy.

So, are you happy love is a mystery now? I thought so, because I figured if you're reading this book, you must be pretty smart and open to new ideas. That's really great. I'm feeling kind of bonded to you right now, and I've never met you, and you haven't even read this yet because I'm still writing it, but I'm imagining you reading it sometime in the future, and I find myself really liking you. Now that's mysterious!

Chapter Two

What Do You Mean,
I'm Not a Billiard Ball??

Help! I'm All Tangled Up and I Can't Get Out!

*L*ove may be a mystery, but the things that get in the way of love don't have to be. Unfortunately, we are often totally confused about why we get all tangled up and tied in knots on the way to true love. For example, someone whom you have been blissfully dating for two years breaks up with you just as you're beginning to wonder where to have your destination wedding. You're about as shocked as the patrons of the pie shop in *Sweeney Todd*[4] when they find out they have developed a taste for human flesh. How could you have been so deceived? You thought you'd been feasting on true love only to find out that the recipe had a seriously flawed ingredient.

So you begin the inevitable search for whom or what to blame by polling your friends, and what you're hoping to hear is that your lover was a jerk and completely to blame for everything. That's probably what they say, or they would be your lover's friends and not yours, but deep in your soul you fear exactly the opposite. What if the faulty ingredient is you? You think, "*I'm* the jerk. *I'm* incapable of sustaining a relationship. What's wrong with *me*? Why doesn't anyone want to spend their life with *me*?" As a kid at summer camp I used to sing a song with the refrain, "Nobody likes me, everybody hates me. I think I'll eat some

---

[4] *Sweeney Todd: The Demon Barber of Fleet Street*, dir. Tim Burton, writ. John Logan, perf. Johnny Depp, DVD, DreamWorks Pictures, 2007.

worms." That about sums it up. You feel confused, not only about what love is but about whether you are capable of love. And so, for a while at least, you confine yourself to a diet of worms, and probably date a few, too.

Before you do further damage to your digestive tract, your chances for love, or your self-esteem, this book is going to teach you how to spot some of true love's more common stumbling blocks. The key to clearing up the confusion about love is to discover the wicked truth about what makes us tick as human beings. After all, it takes two to tango, and the "two" are people – plain old, garden-variety human beings. People are the ingredients of the love pie. Maybe that's the deeper meaning of the *Sweeney Todd* cuisine. Because we don't know enough about what it means to be human, we mistake one another for things that we can consume, cannibalizing lovers as if they were meat pies and not human beings. Okay, that's probably a stretch, but you get the idea – not knowing the truth about ourselves is a recipe for disaster.

What I'm getting at here is that love may be a mystery, but the nature of human nature is not. Yet, the sad reality is we really have no idea what it means to be a human being. Actually, it's worse than that. We have the WRONG idea and not a clue in the world that it's wrong, except for the fact that we keep getting all tangled up on the way to love. But we think we're entangled because we don't have the right things on our love to-do list.

So here's the crux of the problem: we operate under a truckload of misconceptions about exactly how human beings operate. Trying to build a relationship with incomplete knowledge about human beings is like trying to build a bridge without knowing the tensile strength of steel. (I'm told that's a really stupid way to build a bridge.)

It's not our fault that we have this seriously inaccurate knowledge about ourselves – our culture feeds us a steady stream of (mis)information that is nothing more than a bunch of lies and cover-ups. It's all so convincing that we don't even suspect we're being fed a load of horse manure, and so we don't think to look for different or better information.

You can compare what our culture tells us about human beings to the virtual reality in the movie, *The Matrix*.[5] In that movie, average people are living their lives thinking everything is real, but the truth is their lives are nothing more than a computer simulation, and their real bodies are floating in some eerie laboratory hooked up on life support. They're alive all right, but they might as well be dead because everything they think they know is a lie.

Behind the Eight Ball

So let's start unraveling our cultural matrix by challenging its biggest lie: You are not a billiard ball. You may not realize it, but that is what our culture wants you to believe.

Let's take a second to be sure I'm being clear about what I mean by "culture." I don't mean "cultured" like going to the opera, or "culture" like something you grew in a Petri dish in high school chemistry. I mean that culture is the sum total of things in our social environment that we all believe without having to be told what they are or having them explained to us. Like freedom is good or progress is better than no progress or science can explain the world or Elvis makes regular appearances at county road gas stations; stuff like that, that we all tend to agree on and accept as true because everyone else does.

Now back to the pool table: our western, American culture has this idea that human beings are like billiard balls. Each one of us is an individual completely independent of everyone else, as if there were some self, some essential core of who we are that was contained and sealed inside a hard outer shell, like a billiard ball.

[5] *The Matrix*, dirs and writs. Andy Wachowski and Larry Wachowski, perf. Keanu Reeves, DVD, Groucho II Film Partnership, 1999.

All of our desires, dreams, wishes, hopes, and loves spring from this core. Life becomes a process of trying to connect to that core, that authentic self, from which our desires spring, so that we can fulfill them and be happy.

The practice of psychology is about looking deep into our unconscious where our true self resides so we can learn to listen closely to our inner voice and be free to be ourselves. In this (mis)understanding of human beings, interpersonal relations look like balls on a pool table – we crash into each other and career off in various directions, but the core of who we are is never affected by all the collisions.

It's the idea behind the myth of the Cowboy[6], the independent loner who knows who he is and what he wants, the rugged individual who is the master of himself and his world. In our culture, we idealize the autonomous individual and fight like rabid dogs for our individual rights, our freedom of expression, our right to be different from everyone else, to have our own opinions no matter how wacky they may be. Being uniquely ourselves becomes the supreme value, and we will not let anyone tell us who to be, how to think, or what to desire. As the kids say, "You are not the boss of me!" Only I can be the boss of me because only I have access to that essential core of all my hopes, desires, dreams, etc. that is deep within my billiard ball shell.

The idea of the unchanging core is also behind the question, "What do you want to be when you grow up?" Remember that one, how every adult you knew asked it? And you had this sense that the answer was hidden somewhere inside you, and if you could only look deep enough you'd find it. But then you had no idea, so you kept searching your insides till you figured it out, which you hoped would be before you had to declare your major.

[6] Frederick J. Turner, *The Significance of the Frontier in American History*, in John Phelan, ed, *Readings in Rural Sociology*, (Madison: MacMillan Company, 1920) 29-33.

20

The billiard ball idea is also behind the myth of romantic love, which says that there is some supremely fabulous billiard ball-like individual out there who is your destiny, and all you have to do is career around the pool table of life until you bump into him or her, at which point sparks will fly, background music will swell, and you will both live happily ever after.

Contrary to that myth, the wicked truth is that we are not born with some essential "self." As we mature and have "life experiences" (which is a euphemism for "really bad things that happen to you"), we do not connect with the hidden core of our unconscious self because it does not exist. All the blood, sweat and tears shed in discovering this inner-lode stone are futile, because that's just it; we are not set in stone.

Think of a baby, for heaven's sake. There is no solid core of a self in there – an infant is nothing but a blob of burping, sucking, pooping, and crying – a cute blob to be sure. But infants are unconscious bobble-head dolls who are incapable of thought and have not yet developed a self such as we know it. Their only dreams and desires are for prompt food delivery and some object to suck on till their cheeks collapse. But they do have something amazing, something that makes them human babies and not some other animal – they have a talent for becoming.

In other words, they don't have a self yet, but they have the ability to create one. That's right, babies are creating machines, and truth be told, you are still one today. We never lose that talent for becoming that we are born with; we just lose sight of it because as we grow up, the neurons in our brain make more and more connections, building incredible networks of memory and knowledge and experience. In other words, we develop a thinking brain that we use to make decisions, to reason and make judgments, to be smart enough to take a picture of Elvis at the gas station, so we can make a fortune selling it to the tabloids. But it is those incredible thinking brains that obscure our awareness of our talent for becoming. Here's what happens.

Wired for Creativity

Babies have no thinking brain yet, so all they have is their talent for becoming. Since the early 1990s, scientists who study the brain have been calling the wiring in our brain that gives us this talent "mirror neurons."[7] What that means is that when you see some action being performed, let's say eating edamame (soybean pods), your brain is firing away as if you are the one eating the edamame too.

There is a region in our frontal cortex known as F5 that is in charge of planning movements and is active just before you do something, such as reaching for the edamame, parting your lips and catching the pod between your teeth, and so on. Here's the cool part: When you watch someone else doing all those things, just watch without actually moving a muscle yourself, a certain subset of the neurons in the F5 region – the mirror neurons – are firing as if it's your hand, your mouth, your lips, your teeth that are digging into those tasty soy pods.

Don't believe it? The scientists who first discovered it didn't believe it either. They were studying the F5 region in macaque monkeys, and they noticed the subset of neurons firing when the monkeys were watching a researcher reach for a peanut. Here's what they said, "We didn't believe it."[8]

Anyway, scientists are beginning to think that mirror neurons are how kids absorb the things around them. They may account for how children learn everything from language to those unspoken cultural ideas like, "We're all billiard balls," to the dreams and desires of everyone around them, some of which will become their own dreams and desires.

[7] Vittoria Gallese, Luciano Fadiga, Leonardo Fogassi and Giacomo Rizzolatti, "Action Recognition in the promotor cortex" *Brain*, April 1996, 593-609.

[8] Greg Miller, "Neuroscience: Reflecting on Another's Mind," *Science*, 13 May 2005, 945-947.

The Devil Made Me Do It

"The devil made me do it" was a phrase made famous in the 1970s by the comedian Flip Wilson.*

It was a great laugh line because everyone knows the devil can't make you do anything. Especially if you don't believe in a devil, but even if you do, you know that no one can make you do anything you don't want to do. We have free will, the ability to choose for ourselves. Devil or no devil, we can't deny personal responsibility and avoid consequences for our actions with a clever laugh line.

Sometimes when people hear about their talent for becoming, they tell me that it sounds a little bit like a new laugh line: "My talent for becoming made me do it." Not quite as funny, but the point is the same. Am I saying that we have no control over our actions and desires, that we are at the mercy of the influences around us? Are we sponges or are we human beings with control over our behavior? The answer is that it's not a case of either/or. It's both. We are human sponges with two potentials: We can go through life like Manchurian candidates responding to hypnotic suggestions, unaware of the ways we have been programmed by outside agents, or we can learn who and what those agents are and decide for ourselves whether or not to accept, reject or modify the programming.

☞

The Devil Made Me Do It, continued

The thing is we cannot escape being influenced by outside forces. It's the only way we have of forming a personality. But that doesn't give us a pass on personal responsibility. If your talent for becoming causes you to do something you didn't want to do, it's up to you to take charge and take over. Another popular phrase, this one from the Masters of the Universe® toy line,** sums it up nicely. When He-Man heroically vanquishes the evil Skeletor, he raises his sword and shouts, "I have the Power!" Luckily your talent for becoming is not evil, and there's no need for a sword, but you do have the Power to take charge, and there's no excuse for not using it. ❦

The Flip Wilson Show, NBC, 1970-1974.

**Masters of the Universe*, dir. Gary Goddard, writ. David Odell, Golan Globus Productions, 1987.

As babies watch people around them moving their mouths to speak, their little mirror neurons are firing away as if they were speaking themselves. This prepares their brains for initiating their own speech. As they grow, their mirror neurons are sparking as they watch adults eat, drink, get dressed, go on a rant, drool over the latest in flat screen technology, and blow their noses. That's why there's a really old parenting adage that goes, "Do what I say, not what I do." But it's futile, really, because anyone who has ever been a parent knows that kids are not listening to what we say so much as watching what we do. (Unless what we say is pretty foul, and then they are sure to repeat it.)

So rather than being born with a core of self inside a billiard ball shell, we are born with the huge job of mining the world around us for building blocks to build a self. Why haven't you heard about this before? Part of the reason is that as our thinking brains grow and mature, they can be annoyed and jealous by the becoming thing. It seems that our thinking brains suffer from massive insecurity. Maybe it's because they come into their own later, after the talent for becoming has done a ton of work to make you you, so they develop an inferiority complex.

But thinking brains also wield a lot of power, and we're going to look at just how powerful they are in a moment. We all know that insecurity coupled with power is a dangerous combination. So what do our powerful and insecure brains do to us? They convince us that we are billiard balls – that we are all thinking brain without any talent for becoming – and we fall for it. The entire cult of the Cowboy, the autonomous individual, and the romantic notion of the ideally matched set of billiard balls are a direct result of our falling for it.

There's a wonderful bit from *The Simpsons*[9] that illustrates this total failure to recognize our talent for becoming. It's new billboard day and as Homer drives by each one on his way home,

[9] *The Simpsons*, Fox, 12 February, 1995.

we see them go by: English Muffins; Best in the West Barbecue Sauce; and Clown College. At work, we see that Homer has on his desk the English muffins and the barbecue sauce. Surveying the stuff, he says, "Well, I got everything I was supposed to get. I'm not going to enroll in that clown college, though...that advertisement had absolutely no effect on me whatsoever."

Like the rest of us, Homer realizes that advertisements do affect him and while he surrenders willingly to the first two billboards, he is in denial about the effect of the third. But denial is not enough to undermine the power of the billboard. At dinner that night, Homer begins shaping his mashed potatoes into a circus tent and hallucinates his family dancing to clown music holding up billboards for the clown college. Finally, in a fit of righteous anger, he says, "That's it! You people have stood in my way long enough. I'm going to clown college!" As he storms from the table, his son Bart says, "I don't think any of us expected him to say that."

The reason that's funny is because we all know that Homer's desire to be a clown did not arise from deep within him. Even Homer knows that he was manipulated by the billboard, and yet he defends his desire to be a clown as if it were some essential and undeniable part of who he has always been. What we see in this exaggerated way in Homer is something that is true about all of us: all our desires are suggested to us from outside of ourselves, but we don't want to believe it.

This way of thinking about yourself may sound a bit strange, but it ends up explaining a lot of things that you couldn't explain without it. All the love tangles we are going to look at defy explanation unless you understand the talent for becoming. Here's something else that is very hard to explain without it: hypnosis. When we follow the suggestion of a hypnotist, it's because the hypnotist – don't ask me how – gets our thinking brains to turn off, and all that's left is our talent for becoming. We stop thinking and just become. A hypnotist can make us do the most amazing things just by saying it. Isn't that wild? Just by saying, "Be a chicken," we become chickens. That's because our talent for becoming is very open to suggestion, and Homer shows this in the extreme. He is a hyper-mimetic creature and as such, he is highly suggestible, almost as if he is living in a perpetual hypnotic trance.

Our talent for becoming turns us into thirsty little sponges who soak up everything and make it part of ourselves. It's an unconscious process that doesn't need our brains to direct it, which is why Homer is so good at it. Remember, babies don't have brains that can reason and think as we do. The lower brain directs the unconscious things like heart beating, lungs breathing, tummy digesting, so these things go on without our higher brain functions all the time, and so does becoming.

When we are children and our thinking brains aren't very well developed, we interact with everything around us indiscriminately. Children treat the world like a store stocked with the building blocks of self, and there's nothing they won't try out, chew on, or test for durability. Children reach for whatever they can see whether it's in their best interests or not. Their talent for becoming is leading them on a voyage of discovery into uncharted territory, and it's filled with all the risks and rewards of exploration. As children reach for all those things, their goal is to use every object they find to complete their mission of building a self. It's not that they want to grab onto the searingly hot pot handle for its own sake; it's to see what a searingly hot pot handle can contribute to who and what they are becoming. And when they cry in the checkout line at the supermarket as if the will die right then and there if they don't get the Dum Dums® so thoughtfully placed on the bottom of the candy display, that inconsolable lament is an expression of lost opportunity arising from deep within their talent for becoming.

Desire This

The important thing to note here is that the desire for pot handles or lollipops is not arising from deep inside our billiard ball self because, as we said, such autonomous desires don't exist. Desire for an object is suggested to us by something outside of us. With children in the grips of a highly charged talent for becoming, suggestion often takes its most basic form: seeing. Whatever comes into a child's field of vision in such a way as to attract the child's attention will become the object of desire. Advertisers know that our desires come from outside of us, not inside, and so they work hard to get our attention and show us their product over and over again until we think we want it, and that the wanting was our idea, that our deepest self will be fully satisfied, realized, fulfilled, happy – whatever, as long as we just Get That Thing – Dum Dums or diamond ring.

And advertisers know one more important thing about desire – what really gets us interested in wanting something is if someone else wants it first. So they show us fully satisfied, realized, fulfilled, happy people wanting the thing that, should we buy it, will make us fully satisfied, realized, fulfilled, and happy too. Or they hire celebrities, who already have our attention because they seem to have all that fulfillment we want, to model their desire for the thing, so we will want the thing too. I can just feel my F5 neurons firing as I watch that pop star drinking a Coke® or that sexy young starlet swooshing her sleekly conditioned, split-end free, waist-length hair across the screen.

What all this is leading to is the real truth about desire. Desire for a thing is not about the thing at all. It's about acquiring what the thing represents, which is the fully satisfied, realized, fulfilled, happy self of the person whose desire for the thing we are imitating. Remember, what we are talking about is the talent for becoming which kids excel in. They are really not interested in acquiring the things at all, but in developing their self. The things are just outward signs of what they are really working to acquire, which is a fully developed self like the adults all around them seem to have.

As you can probably tell, what I mean by desire is different than what we mean when we say "sexual desire." Sexual desire is a physical drive like hunger and thirst, which arises from and resides within our physical body. Anyone who has ever been ambushed by an unexpected rush of sexual attraction or a craving for chocolate covered bananas knows that physical drives can be irrational and overpowering. When I say "desire," I don't mean these physical drives. I am referring to a longing for wholeness. Desire is the search for a fully developed, whole and content self that we've been talking about, and the thing you need to remember is that the longing almost always attaches itself to an object. When I say desire I mean the longing to be a fully developed self, period. How that longing attaches to the object is what we are talking about here.

Confused? That's because of the lie of the billiard ball again. What I'm talking about – the becoming self – is the complete opposite of the billiard ball self. So take a deep breath, and think of this whole desire thing as a triangle. At one corner of the base of the triangle is a child going about the business of becoming. At the top of the triangle is an adult, say his dad, who is just there, present in the child's life, showing him what a grown-up is like. The child has only outward signs to go on, so let's say this dad is a big baseball fan. Let's make being a baseball fan the third corner at the base of the triangle. What the talent for becoming is going to do is make this equation: I, the kid, want to be a grown-up like dad. Dad likes baseball. Being a grown-up equals liking baseball; therefore, I like baseball.

The Talent for Becoming Triangle
Part 1

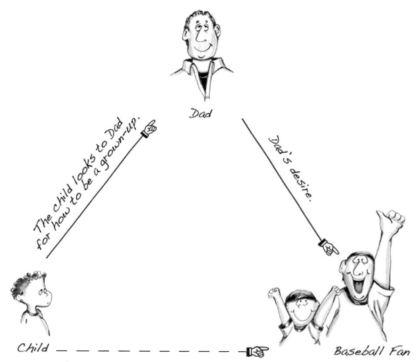

Dad

The child looks to Dad for how to be a grown-up.

Dad's desire.

Child

Baseball Fan

The child equates being a baseball fan with being a grown-up and imitates Dad's desire.

So when Dad is watching the game on TV wearing his team ball cap and telling his kid to watch that great play at second base, the kid's mirror neurons are firing on all cylinders. The kid is learning to imitate the dad's desire for baseball in order to achieve his goal of being a grown-up. It's not baseball he likes so much, as being a grown-up like his dad.

The thing to remember is that the reason the kid likes baseball is not because there is something intrinsically likable about baseball. With apology to the diehard baseball fans out there, the game of baseball itself is value-neutral. The only reason becoming a baseball fan is desirable is because someone the kid loves, respects, and wants to be like makes it so by desiring it himself. Dad could just as easily model a desire for fly fishing, cattle ranching, ballet dancing or slugs. Whatever Dad desires, kid will desire, too. Does that make sense?

Try it with a car commercial. The kid in the previous example is now a twenty-something single guy who wants to date hot women. The Ferrari® in the commercial he's watching is being driven by a dude draped with a bevy of scalding hot babes. Using the logic of the talent for becoming, he thinks, "If I have that car, I'll be draped with a bevy of scalding hot babes."

The truth is our twenty-something doesn't really want the car. He wants to be the dude driving the car with the curvaceous accessories; so his talent for becoming makes the same kind of calculation it did when he was a kid, equating the self he wants to be with the object of desire. We can only hope that during the last twenty years his thinking brain was developing and that it will kick in before he goes into debt to buy a car he can't afford and won't deliver on the new self he thinks he wants.

The Talent for Becoming Triangle
Part II

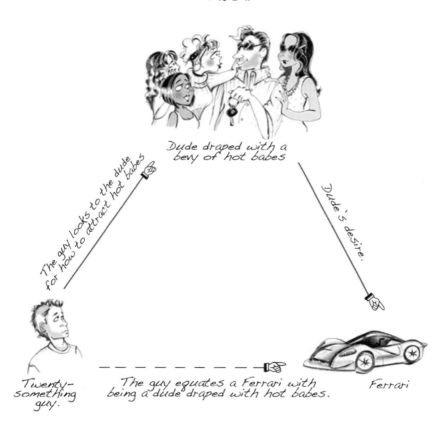

Dude draped with a bevy of hot babes

The guy looks to the dude for how to attract hot babes

Dude's desire.

Twenty-something guy.

The guy equates a Ferrari with being a dude draped with hot babes.

Ferrari

A Freudian Slip

When we talk about triangles, desire, and fathers and sons, we have to acknowledge the most famous example of all, the Oedipal triangle. (You remember Oedipus, the Greek hero who marries his mother by mistake? Sigmund Freud* named one of his most famous complexes after the poor schmo.) Freud's triangle is the worst kind of love triangle there is: the rivalry between a father and son for the same woman. Now that's a love tangle we can all do without. But according to Freud, it's almost impossible to avoid. The best we can do is repress and deny that it ever happened in the first place. Why? Because in Freud's triangle the desire for mom arises spontaneously at an early age in the son, who at the same time is looking to his dad as a model for what a grown-up guy should be. He loves and admires his dad, and he longs to possess his mom. Everything is fine, until – here's how Freud describes it:

> "… until the boy's sexual wishes in regard to his mother become more intense and his father is perceived as an obstacle to them; from this the Oedipus complex originates."**

The poor kid is stuck in a double bind: he wants to be just like his dad, and at the same time, he wants to destroy him, so he can take sole possession of his mother. And his dad is sending messages to be like him in everything except for his relationship with his wife. Yikes! No wonder Oedipus gouged his eyes out. If poor Oedipus was indeed in love with his mom, if any men are

A Freudian Slip, continued

(I don't know any who admit to it, I'll tell you that much), what is really going on has nothing to do with a naturally occurring desire for mom. What Freud clearly understood was that somehow, the son and dad were sharing the same desire and so dad had become both model and obstacle for the son. What he missed was that the son's desire for mom is not there from birth. It was learned from his dad. ❦

*Sigmund Freud, *The Ego and The Id*, supra note 10, at 26- 27 (James Strachey ed., 1960)

**Rene Girard, *Violence and the Sacred*, (London: The Johns Hopkins University Press, 1977) 172.

Talent Isn't Everything

So the bottom line is, and I'm sorry to have to be the one to tell you this, we are not autonomous individuals. We are dependent on others to become who we will be, and just like love being a mystery, that's a good thing.

Our talent for becoming is an astounding gift that makes it possible for us to feel love, compassion and empathy for others. I often think about it as an incredible openness – as if all our nerves were reaching out toward other people like invisible antennae, searching and longing to receive signals from someone, anyone. Like the Mel Gibson character in *What Women Want*,[10] we are as open to one another as if we could read each other's minds. But it's not their thoughts we can read so much as their feelings. That's because we wear our feelings on our faces where we can see them, and they can trigger our mirror neurons.

Scientists have done experiments that show the activity of someone's brain observing someone's face who is disgusted at a foul smell or in pain from receiving an electric shock. The same region of the brain is active in both the observer and the observed[11]. Try this experiment: imagine you are watching someone eat a lemon. Go on, try it. Do you feel your face screwing up? Do you feel your saliva beginning to release? Isn't that weird? Or just smile. Go on, crack a big, wide grin. Don't you feel happier than you did a minute ago? Emotions are contagious. Smiles, frowns, eyes wide with surprise, mouths gaping open in disbelief, brows tight with anger – these expressions trigger our mirror neurons, and in turn, jump start our emotions.

If we weren't so open, we would never be able to understand another point of view. We'd think everyone thought, felt and

---

[10] *What Women Want*, dir. Nancy Meyers, perf. Mel Gibson, DVD, Centropolis Entertainment, 2000.

[11] Greg Miller, "Neuroscience: Reflecting on Another's Mind," *Science*, 13 May 2005, 945-947.

reacted the way we did, and there would certainly be no mystery in that. Sometimes the thing that makes us laugh causes a friend to feel sad. Let's say you're goofing around with peanut butter stuck to the roof of your mouth. You think you're hilarious, but your friend is remembering how he fed his dog peanut butter, and the poor beast choked to death. Being able to read your friend's expression and figure out that he is reliving a bad memory allows you to ask, "Are you okay?" and be open to the possibility that he feels very differently about peanut butter than you do. That's mirror neurons at work.

If we weren't open to others, we could never form attachments to them. We'd have no friends or love relationships because billiard balls don't stick; they just bounce off each other in a lonely existence. We are definitely not billiard balls. We're more like really big squishy, moldable Gummy Bears® who just want to be hugged into new shapes.

What does all this have to do with finding your true love? Since our desires don't arise from inside of us but are suggested to us from the outside, we have to be very careful when it comes to choosing someone to love. We have to be sure that our talent for becoming isn't leading us on a wild goose chase, imitating someone else's desires without any input from our thinking brains.

The talent for becoming is an incredible talent, but it is undisciplined to say the least. It's like a basketball player who can dunk the ball – great talent, right? But if he's part of a team and all he does is hog the ball and try to drive the key to make that dunk, he'll be a lousy team player, and his team won't win many games. He needs a coach who can direct his talent and discipline it, so he can learn when to dunk and when to pass the ball.

The thinking brain functions like a coach for our talent for becoming, directing it to absorb this desire but not that one.

Imagine a virtuoso violinist who wants to be heard above all the other instruments in the orchestra and even insists on playing during the French horn solo. This musician needs a strong conductor who can teach her when to play and when to be silent. That's what our thinking brain can do for us. It is powerful enough to moderate our talent for becoming, preventing it from running wild and indiscriminately absorbing desires and dreams from others. We'll be talking about this more as we explore the six patterns that reveal how we get all tangled up, mistaking other people's desires for our own, but here's an example from my life.

When I was in college, I wanted to date football players. My talent for becoming "logic" went something like this: Football players are hot. Our culture says hot people are worthy love objects. I want someone to love, so I want a football player. I dated a few really good-looking guys on our college football team, but not for long because none of them was quite as lovable as I had been led to believe. This was really not their fault because I was still being led around by my talent for becoming. I met my husband after college, when my thinking brain had kicked in a little, and I realized that what I really wanted was someone to love who would love me. That meant I was looking for a good man and not necessarily a hot football player. Thank goodness, because my husband never played football. He was a hockey goalie, so I would never have dated him in college. We laugh about it now, but it's not really that funny. If my brain had not overridden my talent for becoming, I would have let my husband pass me by, and that would have been a personal tragedy.

To summarize:

- ∝ Love is a mystery, and that's a good thing.

- ∝ We are not billiard balls, but we do have a talent for becoming, which is also a good thing.

∝ Our desires are suggested to us from outside of ourselves.

∝ We need to use our thinking brain, so we don't get all tangled up and mistake other people's desires for our own.

I hope I've convinced you that you're not a billiard ball. I'll give you a couple more examples and experiments that show our mirror neurons and talent for becoming at work just to be sure:

> ✌ The next time you are at a party and the hostess invites the guests to the buffet table, notice how you feel about being the first one in line. Watch how the guests hold back and look at one another, till some brave soul says, "I'll go first," and tries to make a joke out of it. Why do you think this happens? It's because being first means that you are the model for everyone else's desire, and no one is providing a model for you. It's harder to act when there is no action to imitate.

> ✌ What are you wearing right now? How did you decide to buy those clothes? Who or what inspired the look? Is it the clothes you really wanted or the qualities of the type of person who wears clothes like that?

> ✌ I attended a James Taylor concert where someone called out, "I want to be you, James." What musicians, athletes, movie stars or other well-known personalities do you admire? What do you do to be like them?

> ✌ Name a personal goal that you have for your life. Describe how you came to have that goal. Notice in particular the people or ideas that influenced you either positively or negatively.

❧ The next time you are watching TV, notice if you go to the kitchen for the beverage or food just advertised. Do you order a pizza or start craving donuts after seeing a commercial for them? Do you have brand loyalty? Is it really the quality of the product that matters or the image connected to the product?

❧ Why do you drive the car you drive? Is there a different car you'd rather be driving? Why?

Hopefully you noticed in some of those exercises that you have been influenced by others to desire the things you desire, from clothes to cars to life goals. We are always and forever "under the influence" of someone or something, so it's time to accept the truth and stop pretending we are billiard balls. Pretending just causes confusion and unnecessary tangles on the way to being yourself and finding true love.

I just saw Elvis at a gas station, and he reminded me about this song of his called *Change of Habit*.[12] Here's how it goes:

> If you're in old habits
> Set in your old ways
> Changes are a-comin'
> For these are changing days
> And if your head is in the sand
> While things are goin' on
> What you need, what you need,
> What you need is a change of habit.

Being in the dark about your talent for becoming has gotten you into some bad love habits. Let's turn the lights on.

---

[12] Elvis Presley, *Change of Habit*, 1970.

Chapter Three

The Tangles of Desire

The questionnaire in this chapter reveals some of the obstacles to love that many people fall prey to but aren't aware of because we think we are billiard balls. You will most likely fall into one of these patterns, with a smattering from one or two of the others. We tried to design this survey as scientifically as we could,[13] but as we've seen science has its limits. So take the questionnaire, answering as honestly as you can, and feel free to turn to the chapter devoted to your pattern. But I'd suggest that you read the other chapters, too, and see if you recognize parts of yourself in some of them.

This is important: as you read through the patterns, please remember that these are patterns that can be broken. The questionnaire does NOT identify some fixed personality trait of yours that you are destined to live with forever because, sorry to say this again, you are not a billiard ball with a fixed, unchanging self locked inside an impermeable outer shell. The questionnaire is designed to identify a pattern that is, as Elvis says, a little like a bad habit. The good news is that it can be broken and the process can begin without too much effort on your part. Just becoming

---

[13] The attitudinal survey was developed by Ashcraft Research, Inc. The initial survey was conducted online with a representative sample of 450 respondents from a national, geographically representative panel ranging in age from 14 to 39 years with an equal number of male and female participants. Additional responses were gathered from another 708 respondents. This extra series of interviews collected a larger sample of romantic types in order to profile demographically and attitudinally, as well as analyze open end responses from each in the final report.

aware of the pattern will weaken it a lot because you will have let your thinking brain in on the love action. With any luck at all, when you have taken the questionnaire and read this book, the pathway to love will become a little smoother.

For each question, select one response that most closely resembles you. Please read all of the answers carefully before selecting the one that best fits you.

1.) It's Friday night, what are you wearing?

A. I'll have to call up the gang to see what they have on.

B. I'll impress people so much that I'll be the look that defines the year!

C. Something with elegance. But it has to be defiant!

D. I want to walk in the room and make the entire place stand still.

E An outfit that blends me into the crowd. I don't want to stand out.

F. I don't know. I don't think about my clothes very much. Friday night is more about having fun with old and new friends than how I look.

2.) Where are you going tonight?

A. My friends will love that new place I discovered.

B. Wherever I end up, the party always follows. I make the scene.

C. I'm finally getting into that new, exclusive nightclub.

D. I like to go big. I want the VIP treatment.

E. I never want to pick; I leave it up to the others. Whatever makes them happy, that's fine with me.

F. The local bar is OK with me. There are always great people there.

3.) Who did you date in high school?

A. I always had the biggest crush on my best friend's sweetheart. And I knew that I loved them more than my friend did. I could never jeopardize our friendship though.

B. It was the classic tale of beauty and the geek. After a couple weeks with me, I transformed them into a major hottie – everybody wanted them!

C. I went after the unattainable one. My friends said, "You'll never be able to get with them!"

D. I always dated the hottest, most popular one in the school, but was always disappointed. It never lasted.

E. The one I did everything for. I tutored them, showed up to their every game and even changed my college plans for them.

F. We were the on, off, and on again couple. We had some rough times, but we were always able to work things out.

4.) Meeting your lover's parents – What are you expecting?

A. We'll go to a nice Italian restaurant where I can explain how strong and real my love is.

B. If they mention one word about my lover's ex, I'll scream! And I'm keeping a close eye on my lover. If that name is mentioned, there better not be even a flicker of interest.

C. The parents can't stand me! I'm going to do everything in my power to win them over. I'll do whatever
it takes to turn them into believers.

D. Here's my chance to shine! I'll tell them all about
myself and experiences!

E. I'll let the folks decide on the restaurant, even if it
isn't my kind of place.

F. Love me or hate me, I'll do my best to get along
with them.

5.) Ah, the first date. What's in store for tonight?

A. The typical romantic evening topped off with a
perfect kiss goodnight.

B. I have to show off my stunning lover to everybody –
let them see the prize on my arm!

C. I'm going for the kill. I will utterly woo and win
them over. This one date will count for the equiva-
lent of a week's worth.

D. They have to pass my complete examination – any
major flaws, and I'll have second thoughts!

E. I'll leave the ball in their court. It's really up to them.

F. After talking for a while, we realized we both love
music, so we're heading for my favorite live music
spot. I hope it becomes their favorite, too.

6.) The first kiss! How do you make your move?

A. Our first kiss will be filled with passion. I won't be
able to wait till I can tell my best friends about it.

B. I'll set the mood just right – tempting, seductive, tantalizing – they won't be able to resist kissing me.

C. I'll make the move when they expect it least. It'll be a solid smooch that will sweep them off their feet instantly.

D. Quickly, I'll pull them close and lay an R-rated kiss from France on 'em! And if they aren't completely into it, well, au revoir!

E. I'd rather let them make the move.

F. Let's not rush it! It'll happen when it happens.

7.) How would you describe your dating selection process?

A. It all depends on friends. If they pass with them, I'll give it a whirl.

B. I help them become someone that others want really bad. Head-turning, whistles, pickup lines are all stamps of approval.

C. I always find myself going after the one who is trying to get away from me. I enjoy playing the hard-to-get, cat-and-mouse games.

D. I just seek the most beautiful, brightest, successful person on the market. Or rather, they seek me!

E. I fall for the ones who need me most. I pour my heart and soul into every relationship.

F. I put in the dirty work; a relationship needs more than just warm feelings.

8.) Today is the BIG day – your wedding day – the day when *you* stop and *us* begins. How do you feel?

A. I'm marrying my dream lover, who is also my best friend's ex. I am disappointed that my best friend decided not to celebrate with us.

B. This wedding I've put together will be spectacular. Martha Stewart would be jealous.

C. I'm afraid the excitement is going to die after the honeymoon! I don't want to lose the rush.

D. I don't know if I can go through with it. Being with just one person for the rest of my entire life?

E. I want my partner to have the most unforgettable day. I did not lie when I vowed to serve them for the rest of our lives.

F. I am starting the greatest adventure of my life with the person I will promise to love forever.

9.) Your lover is having the absolute worst day of their life. You want to cheer them up. What will you do?

A. I'll set up an especially romantic evening. Nothing does the trick quite like some romance.

B. I hope this doesn't go on for too long. I wouldn't want to be with somebody who brings me down with them.

C. To the rescue! With a little effort I can take care of absolutely anything!

D. I am just about fed up with these bad days! I'll try to avoid them for a while and let things pass by.

F. First, I'll ask them if I can do anything in order to cheer them up. Then I'll do whatever they want.

G. I'll simply just be there to let them vent.

10.) It's time to get away. What kind of weekend vacation do you plan for you and your lover?

A. I would call up my best friends to see if they'd be interested in taking some time off with us.

B. I would suggest a big city trip – New York, Chicago, L.A. I prefer mixing it up with the crowds.

C. Something adventurous – rock climbing, skydiving, whitewater rafting!

D. I want to do something big, maybe an all-inclusive in Cancun. The nightlife is great, and it gives us a chance to strut our stuff on the beaches.

E. I'll plan everything around them. Whatever they like to do, that's what we'll do. Wherever they wish to go, that's where we'll be.

F. I don't want to rush things. Maybe we can make plans in a couple months.

11.) Nobody is perfect. What one thing would you change about your lover?

A. They would be dating me and not my friend!

B. One thing? How about everything?

C. I would change their mind, and I'm going to. They say they don't want me like I want them, but I'll sway their thoughts soon enough.

D. Maybe a little younger, a tad bit hotter. I could always find somebody else that fits the bill.

E. I understand their issues and past and would never ask them to change. If anything, I would be the one making changes in myself to please them.

F. Perhaps they could put forth a bit more energy into the relationship.

12.) If you've got it, flaunt it! What's your most appealing trait?

A. My companionship and closeness to my friends.

B. My irresistible creativity.

C. My determination and drive.

D. That's easy – Me.

E. My enormous, generous heart.

F. My understanding.

13.) If your love life were to be made into a Hollywood blockbuster, what would it be?

A. *Stand By Me.* What a terrific story of true friends!

B. *Striptease.* Hot and spicy and rated R.

C. *Superman.* Leap tall buildings in a single bound and steal the heart of my lover in a single swoop.

D. *The Greatest Story Ever Told.* Of course it'll be about me and my life.

E. *Pay It Forward.* It carries a great message about giving and sacrifices for the sake of others.

F. *When Harry Met Sally.* This story shows how love is a work-in-progress and how to build it.

14.) After a year of a new, steady relationship, your ex-flame moves back into town and is vying for your interest. What do you do? Who do you choose?

A. I ask my friends for their advice.

B. I'm sure to let my current lover know what's up – a little jealousy is good for a relationship.

C. I need some excitement in my love life. I'll go after them both!

D. It all depends – who looks the best?

E. After pouring all I have into that past relationship, I never thought I'd find another. But I have, and now I live and breathe for my current lover.

F. I'll be sure to acknowledge them, but I am working on a steady, successful relationship now.

15.) If you had to choose any famous twosome whom you and your lover most resemble, who would it be?

A. Ross and Rachel of *Friends.* True love keeps trying.

B. Tom Cruise and Katie Holmes. I have so much to teach my lover.

C. Clark Kent and Lois Lane. Here I come to save the day.

D. Pamela Anderson and Tommy Lee. We look great together.

E. Montgomery Burns and Waylon Smithers of *The Simpsons.* Why can't you see how much I love you?

F. Shrek and Princess Fiona. True beauty is below the surface.

16.) Which song best describes the type of relationship you have with your lover?

A. *My Best Friend.* "You're more than a lover / There could never be another."

B. *Jealousy.* "It's much too late/ Where've you been?/ Who've you seen?/ You didn't phone when you said you would!"

C. *Ain't No Mountain High Enough.* "There ain't no mountain high enough/ Ain't no valley low enough/ Ain't no river wide enough/ To keep me from getting to you."

D. *Rock and Roll All Nite.* "I wanna rock and roll all nite and party every day."

E. *(Everything I Do) I Do It For You.* "Ya know it's true/ Everything I do – I do it for you."

F. *When a Man Loves a Woman.* "He'll trade the world/ For the good thing he's found."

17.) Congratulations on your first anniversary! What are you buying for your loved one?

A. A photo album filled with all the special moments we've spent together and with our friends.

B. A complete makeover and a fresh outfit.

C. I managed to find tickets to the sold-out concert of their favorite band.

D. A big, expensive piece of jewelry. And I'd buy myself something nice while I am at it!

E. I would go overboard and buy about ten different things for them. I'm just doing my best to please them.

F. How do you say I love you more each day? I'd find a way to let them know how complete my life is with them.

18.) What kind of car are you and your lover driving around in?

A. Ford Focus. All my friends drive them.

B. Chrysler 300, customized and tricked out of course. Everyone wants one like it.

C. Hummer H3. I'm ready to overcome any obstacle.

D. Porsche 911 Turbo. It's one sexy, hot number that turns heads.

E. Chevy Aveo. No flashy wheels for me.

F. Civic Hybrid. Good for the earth and my wallet.

19.) You get a call from your lover on Sunday afternoon, "Want to hang out?" What do you suggest to do?

A. I'd suggest calling some friends of ours and all of us spending the day together.

B. I say we get done up and hit the swanky restaurant downtown.

C. I suggest some physical activity – hiking, rollerblading, running.

D. I have to apologize because I planned out my entire day with things I want to do. Maybe we can meet up tomorrow when I'm not busy and hang out.

E. I would prefer to call it a "lazy Sunday." I'll cater to their needs and make sure they have a comfortable, pleasant day.

F. Whatever we decide to do, it would be more fun together.

20.) You decide to stay in one night. What dish are you making for your lover and self?

A. A loaf of bread, a jug of wine and candlelight.

B. I'll make something amazing, the perfect first step on the path to seduction!

C. Something new, something I have never made before.

D. Caviar and lobster (don't tell, but I ordered it).

E. Anything they want. Even if I don't like it, I will make it just for them.

F. Something we can make together and both enjoy.

21.) After slamming some shots at the bar, you instinctively shimmy your way to the dance floor. You feel a slight tap on your shoulder and are asked to mix it up with some hottie. Shall we dance?

A. No thanks, I'm here to have a good time with all my friends.

B. First I need my bar mates to check them out. If I get the nod of approval, I'll get down!

C. Sorry, but I have been trying to dance with somebody else all night long.

D. Dance with you? More like you will be dancing with me! And then I'll show them all my moves.

E. I'd do it. I would feel too bad shooting them down and hurting their feelings.

F. It depends on the song really. Maybe I'll give it a go if it's the right beat.

22.) Your loved one approaches you warily and mutters the most horrifying sentence in the modern English language – We need to talk. Nobody *needs* to talk. How do you handle the breakup?

A. It's always nice to have the support from your best friends. I look to them for advice and guidance.

B. I'm angry. After all I've done to make them appealing and desired by others, this is how I'm repaid?

C. I do not go down without a fight. I try everything in order to keep this relationship alive.

D. See ya later! There has to be somebody younger and hotter than them anyways. No worries for me.

E. I beg and plead to keep things afloat. I let them know I'll do absolutely anything to stay together and explain just how much they need me in their life.

F. We'll try to work it out, but if not, it's onward and upward.

23.) Your coworker will not stop hounding you for a date. You've beat around the bush for too long. Your move is...

A. Explain to them that they're too good of a friend and it would be best to remain so.

B. I make a scene and turn them down with flair. I want everyone to know that I don't date just anybody!

C. Interoffice relationships are strictly prohibited.
   I take the date!

D. No way! With all the fish in the sea, there's no way
   I'm settling for one in my own pond.

E. I feel too bad turning them away. I'll go out with
   them.

F. I'd be firm, but understanding. Maybe I can help
   them see that hounding someone is not a good
   tactic with me, or anyone else for that matter.

**24.) You've been seeing this prospect for a week or two
and you're totally into them. Problem is, whenever
you go out, they are always flirting with others. Right
in front of you! How are you going to handle this one?**

A. They're just flirting with my best friends. It's all
   done for some laughs.

B. It makes me jealous at times, but it does let me know
   that I've got good taste.

C. I put an end to it immediately! Instead of getting
   mad at my lover though, I confront the other flirter
   with hostility.

D. I find the nearest hottie and enjoy some flirtatious
   games of my own.

E. It's just flirting – my lover would never hurt me
   intentionally. If that's what they want to do, I'm
   fine with it.

F. I'll keep an eye on it. I know where to draw the line.

25.) Your dream lover is...

    A. Already in a relationship with…my best friend.

    B. My own beautiful, masterful creation.

    C. Impossible to get with (according to others).

    D. Myself (though of the opposite sex of course).

    E. The one who needs me the most in their life.

    F. Not a dream at all. I know lasting love is often unglamorous and involves a lot of hard work.

26.) What kind of effort best describes what you put into your relationship?

    A. It's seemingly effortless. I let the power of romance take care of everything.

    B. I put forth quite a bit of energy trying to make my partner the most presentable I can.

    C. All of my time and energy is spent actually getting into the relationship. Afterwards, the rush is gone.

    D. I don't sweat things. If it doesn't work, then it's on to someone better!

    E. I put everything I am and everything I have into everything I do for the relationship and my lover.

    F. I do what is needed to make things go along. It works that my partner is contributing equally.

Now it's time for the Wicked Truth About Love and to discover the pattern that fits you best.

First, count the number of times you selected a particular response (i.e. if you selected response A twice and response B four times, then you would have two for A and four for B). Next, compare the amounts for all six responses. Match the most frequently selected response number to that of the patterns that follow (i.e. if you selected A most frequently, you fall into pattern A).

Response:	**Times Selected**	**Pattern**
A	_____	Best Friend Forever
B	_____	Celebrity Chef
C	_____	Super Hero
D	_____	Rock Star
E	_____	Sidekick
F	_____	Custodian

Chapter Four

Best Friend Forever

This first obstacle to love, the Best Friend Forever pattern, is what happens when the incredible openness to your friends made possible by your talent for becoming is not regulated by your thinking brain.

Don't be confused by the name "BFF" because this tangle is NOT about falling in love with your best friend. That would be a cool thing. The BFF tangle is about falling in love with your best friend's lover. That is not cool. It's not something we like to talk about, but it does happen.

In movies and on TV, the BFF is often portrayed negatively, as someone who heartlessly betrays the trust of his/her best friend, but that image comes from looking at the BFF from the point of view of the one who has been betrayed. Think of the character Edie from *Desperate Housewives*[14]. Edie is a part of the circle of friends in Susan's neighborhood, but we are given Susan's perspective on everything Edie does, and so Edie comes across as a self-promoting, sexual predator with the morals of a scorpion. Early in the series, Edie pursued Susan's love interest, Mike, and in later seasons she made the moves on the husband of another friend, Gaby. Edie is the classic "frenemy," an enemy masquerading as a friend.

Such a person, if they really existed, would be easy to spot. "Frenemies" have evil intentions, which they are very open about with themselves and which others can see if they want to.

[14] *Desperate Housewives*, ABC, 2004-present.

The "frenemy" conflicts that we read about in the tabloids and fan magazines are manufactured affairs for our entertainment. Real evil is never that easy to identify and rarely hires a press agent to promote itself. But the BFF is not evil at all. When a BFF finds him/herself attracted to their best friend's lover, they are not proud of themselves and will fight the urge as hard as they can. For the BFF, it's not something they are seeking, but it sometimes happens that their best friend's lover seems perfect for them. I mean, you and your best friend are a lot alike, so it just makes sense that the same person would be good for both of you, right?

I have no doubt that it could happen, and here's how our thought process goes when it does. (I'll tell it from a guy's perspective. Gals, use your imaginations.)

"My best friend Carl has fallen hard for Marci, and she is an absolute angel. The thing is Carl doesn't get her at all. He takes her for granted, and I notice that sometimes she seems sad and quiet. It's breaking my heart, really, because I see what a great girl she is. The truth is I am so much better for her than Carl. If he doesn't shape up and start treating her right, I am not going to restrain myself any longer. What I feel is true love, and it wouldn't be fair to any of us for me to keep it inside."

I suppose this could be the complete and accurate explanation for this guy's feelings for Marci; but now that we know that he is not a billiard ball, and his love for Marci is not necessarily something arising spontaneously from inside of him, questions arise that we might want to ask him, like: Are you borrowing your desire from Carl, and mistaking it for your own? Are you using your reasoning brain at all to restrain your talent for becoming, in this case, for becoming like your friend, Carl?

Except for the Nasally Laugh, What do You Think?

Remember Janice, Chandler's girlfriend on *Friends*?*
Chandler couldn't resist her. She was cute, smart, fun-loving, and obviously in love with him. But there was one problem – well, there were a few problems like the fact that she was married, but that's not what I want to talk about here. Janice's laugh annoyed Chandler's friends. I mean really annoyed them so that they couldn't stand to be around her. At one point Joey confessed his utter hatred for Janice, saying that every time she laughs, "I want to rip off my own arm so I have something to throw at her!" Wow, that's a lot of condemnation for one minor quirk. But however irrational, it became a stumbling block for Chandler. It was hard for him to love someone whom his friends didn't love as much as he did. What this clever plot line was getting at is not that we shouldn't want our friends to be welcoming to our significant other; it's how intertwined our desires are with our friends' desires. Even when every instinct in our body is calling us in one direction, as Chandler's instincts were towards Janice, our friends' trivial and self-serving opinions may cause us to doubt our own judgment. Being so tuned into and connected to our friends is also what makes friendships deep and satisfying. So the trick becomes to strike that balance between trusting your friends and trusting yourself. May the Force be with us all. ❣

Friends, NBC, 1994 - 2004.

That is the question that best friends falling in love with their best friend's lover need to ask themselves. It is the question that Imaginary Guy in Love with Marci will never ask because in his normal, everyday relationship with Carl, he checks his thinking brain at the door. Like all BFFs, he has used his talent for becoming to form incredibly close ties with his buddy. These guys most likely have shared taste in things like music, TV and movies. They probably have crushes on the same celebrities. Chances are they're fans of the same teams, the same candidate, the same restaurants. In other words, they share desires. That means that they learn what to desire from one another. When a BFF discovers a new band, s/he will tell her/his friends all about it and see what the reaction is. If it's positive, then the BFF will like the band even more than before. If the friends don't like it, the BFFs excitement over the band will fizzle faster than yesterday's champagne. Sometimes it's hard to know if a tight group became friends because they have so much in common, or they have so much in common because they are such tight friends.

This confusion about "whose desire is it anyway?" causes BFFs to be hopeless romantics. A romantic is someone who only sees two sides of the desire triangle we talked about in Chapter 2. They clearly see themselves and their love object, but the point of the triangle where the model of desire sits is invisible to them, like a mountaintop shrouded in clouds. So BFFs caught in this tangle have to figure out what's going on when they "fall in love" because it really does feel like falling. Suddenly their whole world is spinning out of control, and they are falling hard and fast without any braking mechanism whatsoever.

A BFF searching for love is looking for a magical moment when they will see someone across a crowded room, and snap, in a nanosecond of electrically charged love chemistry, they recognize their true love and live happily ever after. What they don't realize is that the momentary spark is not true love – not yet, anyway – but a match with their ideal of love learned from borrowing desires from somewhere outside themselves. Like what I did when I was dating football players. Maybe the borrowed ideal is a good fit for them – and I say that with a capital Maybe – but unless their thinking brain kicks in and asks the big questions about what is going on here, they will never know for sure.

Our culture is offering us ideal love types all the time that have nothing to do with the type of person who would actually be a good fit for us. We are on the hunt for someone as beautiful and talented as models, movie stars, athletes, and performers because we are taught to equate beauty and acting or sports talent with true lovability, not a very good equation because a key variable has not been identified. I have a friend who likes to say, "Let X equal the unknown," whenever we are trying to make some trivial decision, like where to go for dinner. For romantic types, which the BFF definitely is, X equals the unknown model of their desires. For the BFF searching for love, X is their friend's desire, and unfortunately, it remains a huge unknown to them.

Please don't panic – romance exists. I am not trying to take all the flowers and chocolates and moonlight out of love. In fact, I'm trying to do exactly the opposite. I'm trying to put them in their proper, most deeply meaningful perspective. My hope is that when you open a bottle of expensive wine and plan the perfect evening for your beloved, it will actually be for YOUR beloved and not some mistaken idea borrowed from someone or somewhere else.

Grey's Anatomy of Love

The gorgeous starring couple of the TV melodrama, *Grey's Anatomy*,* Meredith and Derek McDreamy, have run into many romantic difficulties, but they encountered a particularly juicy BFF tangle in season 2. A handsome stranger walked into the hospital and naturally began a seductive conversation with Meredith. Derek watched all this without comment until Meredith reached out to shake the hand of this sexy stranger, whereupon Derek punched the guy in the face. Derek's only comment: "That's Mark." We soon find out that the two men were best friends until Derek caught Mark *in flagrante* with his wife Addison. Mark explains his attraction to Meredith by saying, "Derek and I always had the same taste in women."

Derek's punch was an overreaction to a handshake, but once the juicy gossip is revealed, it's hard to blame him for it. He's right to fear that Mark's casual desire for Meredith will intensify when he learns that Derek and Meredith are a couple. Though Mark has betrayed his friend only once, it's totally possible that this will become a pattern. It's one thing to have the same taste in women and quite another to be willing to wound a friend in order to possess a lover. The expression, "Imitation is the sincerest form of flattery," applies here. Mark's deep and sincere admiration for Derek is the very thing that leads him into the betrayal. He is caught up in the logic of his talent for becoming, which may kick in when he finds out that Meredith is Derek's girl: I want to be Derek,

☞

Grey's Anatomy of Love, continued

Derek has Meredith, I want Meredith. Until Derek is sure that Mark's thinking brain is going to take charge, he'd be a fool to be flattered by Mark's flirtation with his girlfriend. ❣

Grey's Anatomy, ABC, 20 November, 2005.

BFFs have an amazing capacity for love and friendship because they practice the secret ingredient that makes all relationships last – forgiveness. BFFs will forgive each other almost anything. I often think that that's the biggest – maybe the only – difference between a friend and an enemy. You are willing to forgive friends over and over, but not enemies. One mistake from an "enemy" and they are out of your life forever. BFFs truly love and admire one another, but, let's face it, no one's perfect. We make mistakes and hurt one another, often unintentionally, all the time. Even BFFs have misunderstandings, arguments and hurt feelings. If forgiveness doesn't happen in those cases, a BFF can become a WEF (Worst Enemy Forever) in a heartbeat.

This is the risk run by all BFFs in the love arena. Here's what one of the BFFs who took the questionnaire had to say. Let's call her Brenda:

> "I dated one of my best friend's ex's. I didn't realize it at the time, but it really hurt her. Her ex-boyfriend was a friend for a while and then it turned into something more. We were happy, but I lost a friend."

This is a classic BFF situation. We're not sure how the first relationship ended, but we do know that Brenda's best friend was no longer dating this guy, so it seems like an okay move on Brenda's part to go out with him. But once Brenda started dating him, her friend's desire for him seems to have flared up again. Brenda may have borrowed her desire for the guy from her friend, and her friend's desire was reignited when she heard about Brenda's desire. Each one's desire heightened the other's. Sharing likes and dislikes works well when it's for objects or interests like clothes, music, or sports, but when friends share desire for the same lover the capacity for forgiveness is often strained to the breaking point. Brenda lost a friend, and from her use of the past tense – "we were happy" – it sounds like the relationship didn't last either. BFFs need to use their thinking brain to regulate their desires and avoid the pain of a WEF debacle.

The wicked truth is that BFFs are so used to learning what to like from their friends that they cannot help but learn whom to love from them as well. If you are caught in the BFF tangle, your friend's lover will be incredibly desirable to you simply by being chosen by your friend. Your affection for the lover is more like a reflex response than true love – you have been conditioned to love what your friend loves, and so it feels natural and right. But the safest play is just don't go there.

Chapter Five

Celebrity Chef

*W*hen it comes to the desire triangle, Celebrity Chefs gloriously balance at the topmost point as the model of desire. They are masters of temptation, seducing us to fall in love with the things they love (which is okay if you really are a TV Celebrity Chef because you will become rich from the money we spend on your food and your line of ridiculously-expensive kitchen tools that we will never figure out how to use anyway). But if you are a lover who falls into the Celebrity Chef tangle, you are in for a lot of disappointment. Here's why:

TV chefs in their make-believe TV kitchens use visually stunning presentations, exotic ingredients and irresistible flavors to woo us. They want us to fall in love with the things they make; and we do, often finding that we are overcome with cravings for their creations. In fact, we crave being them and go to ridiculous lengths to do our best TV chef imitation in our own kitchens.

Have you ever been invited to dinner by a friend who serves you some crazy recipe she saw on the cable food network? What do you say when it tastes like she seasoned the scallops with fish food? To avoid hurting her feelings, you say, "Wow, it's just like Chef Ooh-la-la took over your body," or something equally ridiculous that you know she wants to hear. But TV Chef Ooh-la-la would be delighted that someone attempted to imitate him. People caught in the Celebrity Chef tangle would enjoy it greatly if we were so jealous of them we went around doing pathetic imitations of them instead of being ourselves.

69

The Turtle Trainer

Most of us have a "pinch" of Celebrity Chef in us. It manifests in subtle ways. Take how we decide what to wear. We choose clothes to project an image that we want others to reflect back to us. Whether we choose stylish and hip, prim and preppie, casual and indifferent, athlete or fan, geekie or goth, we are trying to coax the feedback we need out of everyone we meet.

Samantha pulled a Celebrity Chef on an episode of the HBO series, *Sex and the City*. She had just been dumped and was in serious need of a morale boost when she ran into a guy known as The Turtle. He was quick to give her the compliments she needed, but he was also "a Manhattan legend known for two things: good investments and bad breath." He was the definition of repulsive. Hanging out with him could generate some very negative feedback. Maybe during happier times Samantha could deal with those withering looks and catty comments from her friends, but not so soon after her self-esteem had taken such a blow. So she came up with a (seemingly) wonderful solution to both their problems. She decided to improve The Turtle and bring him up to her level. A quick haircut, teeth cleaning, and new clothes, and *poof*! he became the "perfect" (rebound) guy for Samantha. Here's how she explained it to Carrie:

☞

The Turtle Trainer, continued

Samantha:	Once we get the breath under control, I'm going to take him shopping for a whole new wardrobe. He's a cute little fixer-upper.
Carrie:	Sweetheart, he's a man. Not a Brownstone.
Samantha:	Honey, when I'm through with him, he'll be the Gracie Mansion.

This is classic Celebrity Chef. The need for positive feedback is enormous, and nothing will get in the way of acquiring it, not even treating a human being like a handyman's special. ❦

Sex and the City, HBO, 2 August 1998.

Why does the person caught in the Celebrity Chef tangle need us to be so captivated? Because without our adulation, the Celebrity Chef does not feel confident or good about himself or herself.

Usually, when we are children and our talent for becoming is guiding our interaction with the world, we get feedback from our parents, grandparents, family and friends that we are cute and adorable. We absorb their tender desire for us, and it anchors our sense of our own lovability. For whatever reason, this didn't happen for the Celebrity Chef. Maybe the feedback wasn't there or wasn't strong enough or the Celebrity Chef just didn't believe it. The result is that as adults they still crave that feedback; in fact, they are addicted to it because without admiring glances from outside, they doubt their own lovability.

This doubt is so fundamental to the Celebrity Chef's sense of himself, that to counter it he needs huge displays of admiration. That's where envy comes in because envy is obsessive admiration. People who envy you really do want to take over your body and inhabit your life. For non-Celebrity Chefs though, being the object of envy gives you a creepy feeling. I remember the old *Road Runner*[15] cartoons where the Coyote would be so hungry and so desperate that the Road Runner's body would look to him like a plucked and roasted chicken. When someone looks at you with envious eyes you feel like that stuffed, steamy bird about to be carved up for Thanksgiving.

But Celebrity Chefs don't think being envied is creepy at all. They like to see us drool, especially when it comes to their love choices. They need to be applauded, to hear, "Nice job on picking a lover!" or at least see the approval in our eyes. But that's not the worst of it. They lay a trap for themselves that is worthy of a genius. In order to bolster their confidence and to steady their wavering emotions, they work overtime to make their friends

[15] *Road Runner*, Chuck Jones for Warner Brothers, 1948.

admire their lover – to the point of encouraging and enjoying active flirting by their salivating pals. Like a TV chef waving a plate of steaming lobster-stuffed ravioli in vodka cream sauce in front of the studio audience, the Celebrity Chef wants to make his friends drool over his girl. (Women do this, too, of course.) Nothing delights them more than when their friends show their approval. "She's a looker, Wayne – What's she doing with a guy like you?" Or, "If she ever dumps you, Wayne, watch out, buddy. I'm making my move." On the one hand, Wayne is thrilled that his friends like his girl; but his basic insecurity leads him to wonder, "Do they like her too much? And what if she starts to like one of them back? I mean, do you see the way she giggles and flirts when they drool over her? What's she doing with a guy like me anyway?" That's how the mind of the Celebrity Chef works.

Here's a comment from a Celebrity Chef after taking the questionnaire:

> "I always DO go for the UNTAMED ones, but eventually they start getting flirts with other people, and so they go after them."

What this Celebrity Chef doesn't realize is that by needing the approval of others so desperately, he is actually stimulating their desire for his lover. He's worked himself into the classic double bind: he wants his friends to desire his girl, but only up to a point. He wants them to imitate his desire for her, but not try to take his place and steal the girl.

It's a tough situation for the Celebrity Chef, his friends and his lover. Underneath the Chef's showy, attention-grabbing maneuvers is a big, black pit of doubt. Celebrity Chefs may always steal center stage, but it's because deep down they believe they are losers. They just can't bring themselves to believe that their heart throb really loves them back. They think someone that fabulous who makes friends and strangers look twice couldn't possibly be in love with them.

To keep the doubt at bay, the Celebrity Chef works overtime to keep those admiring glances coming. But this dependency on other people's approval has a huge drawback. What if the envy isn't there or dries up? What if instead of admiring glances, the Celebrity Chef receives empty gazes or shrugs? And what if the Celebrity Chef misinterprets what he's seeing, because that happens a lot. When you see every interaction through a lens that says, "I'm a loser. I need you to envy me. But you'll figure out soon enough that I'm a loser," you really have no idea what is happening inside someone else's head. It's all in your head, and you don't realize that you are creating other people in your own image.

So if Celebrity Chefs don't get the real or imagined response they need, their feelings for their beloved may waver, maybe even dry up all together. And this can change on a dime. One day they may feel deeply in love for all eternity, and the next day, they may be floundering in doubt – all because of the way they interpreted a sidelong glance or offhand comment from a friend. Basically they are insecure, neurotic messes. No one is ever sure what mood the Celebrity Chef will be in and whether his pleasure at having his lover admired will morph into a jealous rage over some trifling incident, leaving everyone to wonder what the heck just happened.

I am a fan of *The King of Queens*.[16] The lead character, Doug Heffernan, is a Celebrity Chef type. He enjoys being married to a woman who is out of his league. While she's thin and gorgeous, he's an overweight underachiever. It boosts his ego to hear his friends wonder aloud how he landed such a hot wife. In one episode, however, Doug is crushed to find out that Carrie slept with a mutual friend of theirs. If I remember correctly, it was

[16] *King of Queens*, CBS, 1998-2007.

before Carrie and Doug were dating, but Doug is upset that Carrie never told him about it. He imagines that everyone has been laughing about him behind his back. His ego is very fragile, and it's obvious that Carrie has broken some unspoken agreement. Her job is to make Doug look good by inciting his friends' desire for her without allowing them to act on it. Doug is walking a thin line – on one side of the line he's his own hero, and on the other side, he's everyone's goat.

Sadly, all this self-doubt can turn into loathing. If the Celebrity Chef keeps all his uncertainties inside, he convinces himself that everything he suspects is true because it is inevitable. If you fall into this tangle, you know that your show of outward confidence is just that, a show. You are sure that no one as wonderful as your lover could really be in love with you, so you tend to sabotage relationships. You might succumb to self-loathing and do the "I'll-dump-you-before-you-dump-me" routine. Or you can turn the loathing outward and accuse your lover of infidelity or your friends of betrayal. You feel isolated and alone and don't believe their protestations. All the fun you had when you were the envy of all you surveyed has turned as sour as curdled milk. The only way you know to get it back is to start all over again with a new lover, maybe even with new friends.

So if you have fallen into this pattern, you will notice you need the approval of others to feel secure about the choice of your lover. You will find that in parading your lover in front of your friends to excite their admiration, you become worried that you may inadvertently awaken their desire to take your place and claim your lover as their own. You may be prone to jealousy and suspicion. Your path to true love will open up when you believe in your own lovability and gain confidence in your own ability to choose lovers wisely.

Zounds, Othello! Simmer Down, Now.

𝒜 Celebrity Chef isn't always obvious about parading his or her lover for admiration. He or she can be much more subtle, hiding deep insecurity behind a confident façade. The first sign that a Celebrity Chef may be his own obstacle to love may be jealousy, what Shakespeare famously described as, "the green ey'd monster which doth mock the meat it feeds on."* Here Shakespeare is comparing envy to the way a cat, often green-eyed, will toy with its prey before it kills it. Sadly, the Celebrity Chef can be a most passionate and intense lover capable of morphing into a love killer over a trifle.

Remember *Othello*** from high school English or the 1995 movie starring Laurence Fishburn? Othello is an up and coming officer who enjoys hob-nobbing with high society. He is a bona fide social climber and an acclaimed military hero, the kind of guy who'd make the cover of *TIME Magazine* today. Othello is delighted when he wins the love of Desdemona, a Senator's daughter, someone he assumed was beyond his reach. His insecurities, however, are soon aroused by Iago, his resentful assistant who has been passed over for promotion. Clever Iago, aware of his boss's frail ego, plants the seed of doubt in Othello, suggesting that Desdemona and young Lieutenant Cassio are having an affair. The proof? Iago claims to have seen Cassio with Desdemona's handkerchief, a gift from Othello. In truth, Iago stole the hanky and planted it in Cassio's apartment. When Othello punishes Cassio for a fight (that Iago also arranged), the young lieutenant asks

Zounds, Othello! Simmer Down, Now, continued

Desdemona to intercede with her husband, which she gladly does. While she is asking Othello to reconsider his punishment of Cassio, Othello pesters her for the handkerchief. Can you detect the insanity behind Othello's jealousy in their dialogue?

Othello:	Fetch me the handkerchief: my mind misgives.
Desdemona:	Come, come; You'll never meet a more sufficient man. (Author's note: She means Cassio)
Othello:	The handkerchief!
Desdemona:	I pray, talk me of Cassio.
Othello:	The handkerchief!
Desdemona:	A man that all his time Hath founded his good fortunes on your love, Shar'd dangers with you –
Othello:	The handkerchief!
Desdemona:	I'faith, you are to blame.
Othello:	Zounds! (Exit Othello.)+

As soon as Othello leaves, Desdemona's maid asks, "Is not this man jealous?" Zounds! He's out of his mind with jealousy! Each time Desdemona wants to talk about

☞

Cassio, Othello interprets it as proof that she is having an affair. And the fact that she can't produce the handkerchief, well, call in the DA – what more proof do we need? You may remember that this is one of Shakespeare's tragedies – Othello ends up killing Desdemona, the woman he loves dearly. Unable to live with his grief, he kills himself as the play ends. The real tragedy is how easy Othello was to deceive, and how simple it would have been to avoid all the drama. Because of the Celebrity Chef inside of him, Othello found it more likely that Desdemona would betray him than that she would love him. ❣

Othello III, iii, 189-91.

**Othello* dir. Oliver Parker, writs, William Shakespeare and Oliver Parker, perfs Laurence Fishburne, DVD, Castle Rock Entertainment, 1995.

+*Othello* III, iv, 101-111.

Chapter Six

Super Hero

Super Heroes thrive on impossible odds. The more dire the situation, the more powerful the opponent, the greater the risk to life and limb, the more determined the Super Hero. No obstacle is too great to prevent the Super Hero from saving the day. And once the day has been saved, the Super Hero vanishes to a secret hideout until the next disaster looms. It's as if the Super Hero doesn't exist at all unless there is a hurdle to leap. We can wonder which the Super Hero loves more – doing good or overcoming obstacles; because if doing the good thing were easy, the Hero wouldn't be Super anymore.

For the Super Hero lover, conquering impediments to love is the name of the game. The more impossible the odds stacked against acquiring a certain lover, the more desirable that lover will become. Maybe the lover is "out of my league" or forbidden by family or looks upon the Hero with disdain – all the better! Somehow the Super Hero lover has confused love with impossible odds. How did that happen?

Not surprisingly, it has to do with that desire triangle again. Remember the dad at the top of the triangle and the kid learning how to be a grown-up by imitating Dad's desires? Well, imagine what happens when the dad has something he really treasures, like his baseball from the 19XX All Star game with Mr. Batting Champion's autograph on it. He shows it to his son, and the little kid in all his innocence asks, "Can I hold it?" Dad nearly turns purple and spits cleats. "Not on your life, kid," he tells him. "Don't ever touch this ball, don't ever play with it, never ever."

And The Winner Is... The Loser

You're single, perched on a barstool and surveying the likely prospects. How do you decide whether or not you "stand a chance" with someone? Do you rate the likelihood you'll be snubbed by ranking your attractiveness against theirs ("He's a 9; I'm just a 6 on good days"), by comparing clothing, drinks, or who they're hanging with? Most of us try to assess the odds of rejection and go after safe bets, confining our flirtations to targets "in our league," as the expression goes. But what about people who deliberately pursue the one who is obviously out of their league? Are they looking for a safe bet of rejection?

Both Will Hunting and his friend Chuckie in the movie *Good Will Hunting** are Super Heros. Will and Chuckie are working class guys in a bar trying to pick up Harvard co-eds, and Chuckie at least has a plan. When they spot two "Harvard hotties" on the other end of the bar, Chuckie loses his Boston accent and pretends to be what he is not – a Harvard intellectual. Will inconspicuously situates himself closer to listen in as his buddy "works his magic." It would be magic indeed if Chuckie didn't get caught in his lie, when some cocky, for-real Harvard intellectual named Clark steps in and shows him up. Clark provokes Chuckie into giving specifics, "What class did you say that was?" he asks. Chuckie's lame answer is "History." "I remember that class," Clark replies. "It was just between recess and lunch." Burn! Though Will works as a janitor at Harvard, he is a math-

82

ematical genius and has no problem one-upping the guy who is trying to one-up his buddy Chuckie. After his display of intellectual prowess, one of the co-eds gives Will her number, a tangible sign of victory, and Will does not resist the chance to deliver the return burn. In the next scene, he sees the Harvard guy through a window of a Dunkin Donuts® and asks if he likes apples. "Yeah," he says. Will slams the piece of paper with the girl's phone number against the window for him to see and says, "Well, I got her number. How do you like them apples?" Victory is Will's and so is revenge. Now what?

In classic Super Hero fashion, Will has conquered the obstacles and won a prize, the pretty co-ed who admires his brain. But it turns out that Will has a fear of abandonment, and so what he is actually pursuing is not a relationship at all, but failure. Since he believes that someone will inevitably abandon someone, Will wants to be the first to play that card. That's the Super Hero paradox: the intense devotion to the pursuit is often coupled with an equally intense desire to fail. It is one reason why if a Super Hero does succeed in the hot pursuit of the unattainable, their passion soon fizzles. Hidden behind the masks, capes, and leather boots of Super Heroes like Will is an inability to connect as one human being to another. Nothing will change until they remove the mask and reveal their true fears to their lover and to themselves. 💗

* *Good Will Hunting*, dir. Gus Van San, writs. Matt Damon and Ben Affleck, perfs. Robin Williams, Matt Damon, Ben Affleck, DVD, Be Gentlemen Limited Partnership, 1997.

So the son learns, "The more vehemently my dad tells me 'no,' the more desirable the thing is." It's not like this guy is a bad dad – we all do it. The things we treasure are the things we want others to admire; we just don't want to have to share them. The situation is similar to the double bind of the Celebrity Chef, but whereas the Celebrity Chef is in the model's place like the dad, the Super Hero is the kid zeroing in on what his model desires the most.

If the kid grows up into a Super Hero, he will give his potential lovers degree-of-difficulty ratings: the higher the difficulty, the more desirable the lover must be. The movie, *Fools Rush In*,[17] with Matthew Perry and Selma Hayek, does a good job of illustrating this. The Perry and Hayek characters have a one-night stand, but the lustful attraction fades in the harsh light of morning. Isabel, Hayek's character, discovers that one night was all it took to become pregnant, and when she meets Alex, Perry's character, three months later, he wants to do the "right thing." The comedy that ensues is one obstacle after another to not only the wedding itself but to the hopes that their life together will be a happy one. The more extreme the obstacles, the more intense Alex's desire to be married to Isabel becomes. It's as if the challenge itself convinces him it's the right thing to do; so much so that Isabel protests, "Love is a gift, Alex, not an obligation" – a very clever thing to say, for Isabel knows that Alex is caught in the Super Hero pattern. He is confusing love with hardship, and until he gets it untangled in his own head, she will never be sure whether he loves her for herself or for the challenge she represents.

[17] *Fools Rush In*, dir. Andy Tennant, writs. Joan Taylor, Katherine Reback, perfs. Matthew Perry and Selma Hayek, DVD, Columbia Pictures Corporation, 1997.

Prince Charming to the Rescue

 ou name the fairy tale with a princess who needs rescuing, and I'll show you a prince caught in the Super Hero tangle. Snow White, Sleeping Beauty and Cinderella are the big three of the princess set and all represent some huge challenge to be overcome in order to find – or be found by – their true love. Prince Charmings never doubt that the Princess is madly in love with them – they are Super Heroes with super egos. Take the Princes who rescue Snow White and Sleeping Beauty – they fall in love with women in drug-induced stupors. I don't mean to be cynical, but just hearing that Sleeping Beauty was guarded by a forest of thick, tangled briars seemed to get the Prince all hot and bothered. He never stopped to wonder if she would be as enamored with him as he obviously is with himself. And I was never sure if the Prince who pursues Cinderella loved her or her taste in ball gowns. Maybe he only wanted to find her to find out the name of her designer – and if they made glass slippers in men's sizes.

I used my intuition about the Prince Charming type when I was a freshman in college. I was in a room full of freshmen co-eds like myself, all fawning over two dreamy athletes who had wandered into our dorm and flopped onto a bed. The girls were literally sitting at the feet of these guys, giggling like, well, like schoolgirls. I looked around and realized that I had to find a way to separate myself from the crowd, so I left. I stood up, and without saying a word, I left the room and I got immediate results. One of the guys called me that night. The

Prince Charming to the Rescue, continued

Prince Charming side of him was intrigued by my ability to tear myself away from his magnetic presence. And the Super Hero in him responded to how I had made things harder for him by leaving the room and feigning disinterest. The relationship lasted all of four months, which is fairly long when you consider that I had manipulated him into asking me out. He was obviously more fascinated by his own power to fascinate than in me and without my shameless tactic, I doubt he would have noticed me at all. If you are a princess looking for happily ever after, I'd suggest chopping the briar forest down yourself. Maybe someone has been standing on the perimeter waiting to be discovered. ❦

A big danger here is that the Super Hero lover will fall in love with people who disdain them. In fact, the disdain may feel like a pre-requisite to love. The more someone pushes them away, the more intense their desire for that person becomes. For the Super Hero, "No" means "Yes." If they are not careful, they can become the annoying lover who won't take no for an answer, or in the extreme, an obsessed stalker. Think of Glenn Close in *Fatal Attraction*.[18] Not an attractive place to be.

One sure way to know if you have fallen into this pattern is to observe what happens when you have conquered all obstacles and won the heart of your lover. Does the thrill last, or does it fade almost overnight? If it fades, the pursuing of love is far more exciting to you than actually being in love, so you fall out of love almost as soon as you have won the day. A Super Hero who took the questionnaire summed it up quite nicely: "100% true. I chase, then once I get, I get rid of." If you fall into this tangle, your path to true love will open up when you realize that the degree of difficulty in a relationship is not a reliable measure of true love.

[18] *Fatal Attraction*, dir. Adrian Lyne, writ. James Dearden, perfs. Glenn Close and Michael Douglas, Paramount Pictures, 1987.

Chapter Seven

Rock Star

The Rock Star tangle is a manifestation of a big mistake we make from our seat at the base of the desire triangle: we get confused about how our talent for becoming connects us to the objects we desire. In other words, we forget that possessing the object and possessing a self are not the same things.

The talent for becoming logic says that the self we want can be transmitted to us through the object, a kind of self-fulfillment ray that will penetrate us as we wear the shoes of Michael Jordan or swing the club used by Tiger Woods or have the same hair color as Heather Locklear. It's as if dress-up were not a game, but something real that can happen to you. Believe me when I say, it doesn't work. I have the shoes, the clubs, the cute skirt and the fancy golf bag owned by every professional woman golfer, and I still can't hit a five wood more than thirty yards. (That's really pathetic.)

So here's what happens to the Rock Star types as they search for true love. Rock Stars are the kind of folks who thrive on being center stage. They are a lot like Celebrity Chefs in this regard, but they don't have to work as hard to grab all the attention. They feel that they deserve it, since they are always the most talented, interesting, and desirable person in the room. They are overdosed with self-confidence and a large helping of charisma, so they believe that they possess a quality of being that no one else has but everyone else wants. Rock Stars allow people into their presence the way kings and queens grant an audience, permitting others to share in their reflected glory.

But like Celebrity Chefs, Rock Stars are not as secure as they seem. Whereas Celebrity Chefs are focused on their admirers, Rock Stars tend to fixate on the objects of desire. They have made the mistake of equating objects with a real self, so in order to keep that self-confidence high, they surround themselves with lots of objects as proof their self even exists.

Think of a real (stereotypical) Rock Star who accumulates things as evidence of status. Gold records, gold jewelry, expensive cars, mansions equipped with recording studios and bowling alleys and movie theaters – these are the outward signs of the Rock Star's inner worth. In quiet moments, however, the Rock Star wonders what would happen if s/he lost all those outward signs. Would the friends and admirers be lost as well? It's hard for the Rock Star to trust that his friends and lovers love him for him and not for his things.

The unfortunate thing for the Rock Star's lovers is that the Rock Star treats them like just another prized possession. The Rock Star's insecurity leads him to evaluate every human being in terms of what they can do for him. Lovers are possessions who either elevate or diminish the Rock Star's ego, but rarely does the Rock Star see that his lovers might have needs of their own.

One Rock Star who completed the questionnaire said, "Everything has to be done my way and I mean everything!" Most Rock Stars are like this because they can't imagine any other way of doing things, and if they did, any other way would be just plain wrong. Or stupid. Or both. I guess we could say that Rock Stars are self-centered and selfish, but it might be more accurate to say that they are self-starved and self-deprived. This makes them needy and greedy to acquire the wholeness which they lack. The Jungian analyst, Judith Pickering, says "… It is not love-as-desire that causes suffering, but love based on selfish desire."[19]

[19] Judith Pickering, *Being in Love* (New York, NY: Bantam Books, 1970) 34.

Can't Buy Me Love?

Rock Stars didn't invent the idea that the more things you have the more love you can attract. Our culture of materialism is in love with the pursuit of possessions. It reinforces the idea that money can buy anything, even love. So here are three ways to remember how foolhardy that belief is, especially if you think that acquiring things will get you more than just an attic full of stuff.

Can't Buy Me Love*
Can't buy me love, love
Can't buy me love

I'll buy you a diamond ring my friend
    if it makes you feel alright
I'll get you anything my friend
    if it makes you feel alright
'Cause I don't care too much for money,
    money can't buy me love

I'll give you all I got to give
    if you say you love me too
I may not have a lot to give but what I got
    I'll give to you
I don't care too much for money,
    money can't buy me love

Can't buy me love, everybody tells me so
Can't buy me love, no no no, no

Say you don't need no diamond ring
    and I'll be satisfied

Can't Buy Me Love?, continued

Tell me that you want the kind of thing
    that money just can't buy
I don't care too much for money,
    money can't buy me love

The Dog and His Shadow, an Aesop fable**

A dog was given a fine meaty bone by a friendly neighbor. On his way home, with the bone firmly between his teeth, the animal had to cross a bridge over a narrow stream. When he reached the middle of the bridge the dog paused to look into the water and saw his own reflection magnified. Thinking that the other dog had a larger bone, the animal decided to take it by force. He leaned over and snapped at his own reflection. As he did so, the bone between his teeth fell into the water and was lost.

Magic Penny+

Love is something if you give it away
You've got to give it away
Give it away
Love is something if you give it away
You'll end up having more

Love is like a lucky penny
Hold it tight and you won't have any
But, give it away
And you'll have plenty
You'll end up having more ❧

*Lennon/McCartney, *Can't Buy Me Love*, 1964.

**William R. White, *Stories for Telling* (Minneapolis, MN: Augsburg Publishing House, 1986) 110-111.

+Malvina Reynolds, *Magic Penny*, 1955.

The Jack Nicholson character in the movie, *Something's Gotta Give*,[20] is a classic Rock Star. A sixty-three-year-old movie industry executive who refuses to date women his age, he is completely dependent on having a trophy girlfriend or two or three on his arm to feel good about himself. He thinks he's living the perfect life and is proud of his ability to attract women. When he is introduced to the mother of one of his sweet young things, she is told that he was once engaged to Diane Sawyer. He assumes that the older woman, played by Diane Keaton, is going to be smitten, bragging, "Women your age love that about me."

Love is nothing more than a game to him, until Diane Keaton's character falls for him and expects him to hold up his end of a real, grown-up relationship. Surprised by his own feelings for her, he panics. When she becomes engaged to a sweet young man of her own, Nicholson's character undertakes some serious soul searching and faces the painful truth that he wounded the women he used to boost his own ego. He actually begins to see them as people instead of possessions. This movie has a happy ending, illustrating that though the path out of the Rock Star tangle is a painful one, the result is a chance at real love.

Here's another trap in the love thicket that Rock Stars get caught in: because their lovers are an outward signs of inner worth, the lover has to be perfect, no flaws allowed. If there is a flaw in the lover, the Rock Star equates it with a flaw in himself, and that is intolerable and way too risky. If all his friends really do love him for his possessions, then the surest way to lose those friends is to have flawed or worthless possessions. Rock Stars don't actually fall in love with someone – they fall in love with someone's perfect looks, wealth, image or reputation. Woe to the lover with a hang nail!

[20] *Something's Gotta Give*, dir and writ. Nancy Meyers, perf. Jack Nicholson and Diane Keaton, DVD, Columbia Pictures Corporation, 2003.

The Modelizer

One *Sex and the City** episode identifies a subset of the Rock Star tangle: modelizers. This is a guy who will only date leggy, impossibly thin fashion models. Not women who look like fashion models, mind you. Modelizers will only date the real thing. Even though the four *Sex and the City* women are real-life cover girls, in this episode they experience the collateral damage suffered by women when they look at themselves through the eyes of a modelizer. Listen to how low their self-esteem drops as they ponder the modelizer's obsession with extreme beauty:

Miranda: Since when did men decide only to get it on with giraffes with big breasts...We should just admit that we live in a culture that promotes impossible standards of beauty.

Carrie: Yeah, except men think they're possible.

Charlotte: I just know that no matter how good I feel about myself, if I see Christy Turlington I just want to give up.

Miranda: Well, I just want to tie her down and force feed her lard. But that's the difference between you and me.

Carrie: What are you talking about? Look at you two. You two are beautiful!

☞

The Modelizer, continued

The girls all mention the body parts they hate about themselves and Samantha finally says, "Hey! I happen to like the way I look!" Then we hear Carrie's voiceover:

Carrie: Suddenly I was interested. If models could cause otherwise rational individuals to crumble in their presence, exactly how powerful was beauty?

What Carrie doesn't realize is it's not beauty that wields all that power. And it's not the modelizer, either. The power resides dynamically with the girls themselves. Despite their protests, the girls are modeling their idea of beauty on the modelizer. Their talent for becoming is magnetically drawing them towards these guys – don't ask me why they find them compelling, but they do – and they are adopting the modelizers' standard of beauty as their own. They are even adopting the modelizers' opinion of them as their own, craving the modelizers' approval in order to feel good about themselves. Oddly, the girls are as obsessed with the modelizer as the modelizer is with models. Carrie does understand that what's needed here is a big dose of rationality, or as we have been talking about it, the girls need their thinking brains to kick in. While condemning the modelizer for sleeping only with models, the girls would do well to be more mindful of the models they are allowing to take up residence in their heads. ❦

Sex and the City, HBO, 6 June 1998.

Like the characters on *Seinfeld*,[21] the Rock Star can become disenchanted and even fall out of love because of the discovery of a trifle that might be construed as a flaw in his lover. The Seinfeld crew found all kinds of excuses to end relationships – big hands, whispery voice, close-talking, and so on. It's because they were, despite their hilarity, what we call "shallow" people. Here's how a Rock Star who took the questionnaire described an uneasy feeling that he might be one of them:

> "I noticed that when in a relationship, that friends are
> very judgmental about what happened. I guess I should
> find people for friends that like the person inside…
> But maybe there isn't much inside to like? I guess
> I need to take another look at myself."

This Rock Star's friends were probably criticizing him for using his lovers as objects. He may even have been doing the classic Rock Star stumble: finding a peccadillo to end the relationship. If he does "take another look at [himself]," he may avoid the "midlife crisis" that often besets aging Rock Stars, the out-with-the-old, in-with the new divorce and remarriage that is really a desperate attempt to find a younger, more "perfect" lover.

If you fall into the Rock Star pattern, your path to true love will open up when you recognize that your inner worth cannot be diminished or increased by outward signs and that you must not use others as objects to enhance your reputation. Then you will be able to choose a lover for their inner worth who will lovingly recognize your own.

[21] *Seinfeld*, NBC, 1990-1998.

Chapter Eight

Sidekick

*D*id you ever hear the expression, "Love hurts"? It sure applies when someone you love lets you down or breaks your heart. Nothing hurts more than that. Your whole body aches from your gut to your fingernails. Then there's this one: "We only hurt the ones we love." I'd rephrase it to say we can only be hurt by someone we love because if we don't care what other people say or do or think about us, how can they hurt us?

Somehow Sidekicks have made a tragic mistake about the relationship between love and being in pain. They think they are the same thing. For Sidekicks, the sure sign of being in love is that they have to work really hard at it. They think their lover should make lots of demands or be extraordinarily needy and consume all their time, energy and emotion. If their lover exhausts them, Sidekicks are sure they've found the real thing.

Nicholas Cage's character in the movie, *It Could Happen To You*, [22] is caught in the Sidekick tangle. He is a cop named Charlie married to Muriel, his high school sweetheart, but they have grown far apart. Loving her is not easy. In fact, he seems to have fallen completely out of love with her, but Charlie is so honest and loyal that the thought of leaving her doesn't occur to him. His unhappiness is something he accepts without question until his fortunes change. The lottery ticket that he promised to split

[22] *It Could Happen To You*, dir. Andrew Bergman, writ. Jane Anderson, perf. Nicholas Cage and Bridget Fonda, DVD, TriStar Pictures, 1994.

with a waitress if he ever won, turns out to be worth $4 million. The money and his commitment to sharing it with the waitress cause the differences between Charlie and Muriel to deepen. Even as Charlie falls in love with the waitress, he cannot leave Muriel. The movie offers us a happy ending by having Muriel leave Charlie because she could see that her happiness and Charlie's would not be found together.

Now, Charlie's determination to stay married to Muriel is not altogether a stupid mistake. He is onto something important about love: sometimes being in love means putting someone else's happiness ahead of your own. In fact, if you haven't learned (1) how to realize that someone has different needs than yours and (2) when their needs conflict with yours, their needs might come before your own, then you are not capable of a truly loving relationship.

Sidekicks have enormous hearts and are incredibly intuitive about what other people need. They live to serve and get real joy out of helping those around them be successful. They don't need the spotlight but celebrate when the spotlight shines on their family or friends. Their favorite phrase is, "Please, let me help."

When Charlie, the cop, is injured helping a storeowner during a robbery, the city gives him a medal for heroism. Embarrassed by all the attention, he donates some of his millions to a fund for injured police officers and their families. Now that's a really nice guy. Like all Sidekicks, Charlie is willing to sacrifice his own happiness to make someone else's dreams come true. All of this is incredibly wonderful. Sidekicks are close to being the perfect lover – for someone else. The problem is, as good as they are about sacrificing for someone else, that's how bad they are at taking care of themselves.

Give Till It Hurts?

Remember the children's story *The Giving Tree* by Shel Silverstein?* Most people think it's a book about love, but I think it's a book about desire. There are only two characters in the story: a boy who grows to be a man and a tall, majestic tree that "grows" to be a dead stump. The tree is systematically consumed by the boy's endless appetite for things: a place to play, money, a house, a boat. The downfall begins when the tree gives the boy apples for money; until he wants something else, which she gives him again. One by one, he strips her of fruit, branches, and ultimately her sap-bearing trunk. The Giving Tree generously but unwisely feeds the boy's endless, unsatisfied desires. Now an old man, the boy returns to the stump he has created. But before her "friend" can express his latest desire, the tree apologizes: no matter what he wants now, she knows she cannot give it to him. But the old man says, (I'm paraphrasing), "You can be the spot where I rest my tired old butt." He plops his sorry self down on the stump, and the book ends with, "And the tree was happy." Really? And even more strikingly, no such claim is made for the man.

For Sidekicks, this tree is their role model, a superstar giver who puts no limits on what she will do for someone she loves. Sidekicks often end up in relationships with people like the boy who take and take and take without ever being satisfied. Sidekicks, like the Giving Tree, need to learn when it's appropriate to say "Ouch!" loud and clear. Noble and caring, generous to a fault, the tree only wants to make the boy happy, but he never is.

Give Till It Hurts?, continued

Swing from my branches and be happy. . . .Use my limbs for a house and be happy. . . . Cut down my trunk for a boat and be happy. . . . All that self-sacrifice does not make him happy and it never will. Perhaps if she had let the boy see how much it hurt to lose her branches, she could have awakened something in him that seems to have never taken root – compassion. The boy, so focused on serial desiring, is blind to the destruction he wracks and to the truth of his existence. He never realizes that it's not the money nor the house nor the boat that can make him happy, but the recognition that he is loved.

Sidekicks must learn to say "Ouch!" and demand that the one with saw in one hand and branch in the other say, "Did that hurt? I'm so sorry. Let me make it better." Better yet, Sidekicks must learn to cry foul before the saw touches the wood. If the story doesn't unfold that way, then the Sidekick can be sure of one thing – there will be no happy ending. 🍂

*Shel Silverstein, *The Giving Tree* (New York, NY: HarperCollins Publishers, 1964).

102

Here's the essence of the Sidekick tangle: Sidekicks need to be needed more than they need to be loved. Being needed and making sacrifices may cause suffering, but the suffering lets Sidekicks know that they have done something extraordinary for someone else, and that makes them feel necessary, as if that other person couldn't get on without them.

There is a certain kind of suffering that Sidekicks cannot endure, however. It's the suffering that comes from "tough love." If the sacrifice that is required to help someone is to say no to them in some way (as in, "No, you can't have another drink and the keys to the car," or "No, you can't use my head as a punching bag even though it makes you feel better"), Sidekicks can't bring themselves to do it because it would mean sacrificing their sense of themselves as endlessly giving. And more importantly, they run the risk of severing the dependency that is so essential to them, the sense that they are needed by someone else. In its worst manifestations, the Sidekick is the enabler to an addicted person. If you say no to someone, they might just say, "To heck with you, then. I don't need you anymore," and that's the Sidekick's worst nightmare.

Here are some comments from Sidekicks who took the questionnaire:

"Well, I gave everything to this one boy. I gave him what he wanted, and offered him everything. If we would of gotten together I would of given him the world and nothing less, but I'm sure I would of gotten nothing from him. I still love him though."

"I do give my all in all relationships and always find I'm getting close to nothing in return."

"I always put my whole heart into relationships and I always end up getting run over in every one of them."

"I like to be in the background and push others into the spotlight. I always find I contribute more in a relationship, leading me to be unhappy."

Don't they sound like wonderful people? It's heartbreaking that they get taken advantage of. For Sidekicks, love really does hurt all the time. These sweet people have to be very careful that they do not fall into abusive relationships. If you fall into the Sidekick pattern, your path to true love will open up when you learn to recognize the difference between self-sacrifice in a healthy relationship and suffering that is unnecessary and unjust. Choose lovers who will not only accept your sacrifices with a spirit of gratitude, but will offer their own sacrifices in return.

The Gloomy Place

In the 1984 Orange Bowl, with six seconds left on the clock and the ball at midfield, Boston College was down by 4 points against Miami.* That's when the Boston quarterback let fly a Hail Mary pass, and every Boston fan crossed every body part available for crossing. What happened next is part of college football lore: the pass was caught and Boston won with time expired. Ask any guy to name the quarterback, and he'll tell you in a heartbeat – Doug Flutie. But ask him to name the receiver, and he'll probably draw a blank, unless he's a die-hard BC fan.

What has football got to do with love? Just like the overlooked receiver (who was Gerard Phelan, by the way), the receiving end of love is an unsung hero. We say, "It is better to give than to receive," but to complete an act of giving, someone has to be there to receive it with sure hands and an open heart. Developing our talent for receiving is essential to being in a loving relationship.

Eyeore, the down-hearted donkey from the *Winnie the Pooh* series, needs a trip to training camp to develop his receiving skills. He tends to wander through the Hundred Acre Woods head-down and muttering things like "Why?" and "Wherefore?" never quite figuring out why or wherefore anyone would want to be his friend. He expects the worst and is always terribly surprised when something good happens. He is so down on himself that he actually lives in a part of the woods called

"Gloomy Place." In the story called *In Which Eyeore Has a Birthday and Gets Two Presents*, he starts his birthday assuming that everyone has forgotten him. Here's how the story begins:

"Eeyore, the old grey Donkey, stood by the side of the stream, and looked at himself in the water.

'Pathetic,' he said. 'That's what it is. Pathetic.'

He turned and walked slowly down the stream for twenty yards, splashed across it, and walked slowly back on the other side. Then he looked at himself in the water again.

'As I thought,' he said. 'No better from this side. But nobody minds. Nobody cares. Pathetic, that's what it is.'"**

You would think that Eyeore would never be able to receive love from anyone; he's so full of self-loathing and self-pity. But what's wonderful about this story is that by the end, when Pooh and Piglet bring him some truly pathetic gifts – an empty honey pot and a popped balloon – Eyeore receives their presents with the innocence of a child. He is able to leave his personal "Gloomy Place" and receive his friends' affection. I don't know how he does it, except that maybe the secret is in his childlike ways. He doesn't judge, simply accepting what is offered at face value.

The Gloomy Place, continued

We all get stuck in our own "Gloomy Place" from time to time, unable to receive love because our imagination has failed us: we cannot imagine how someone else could love a donkey like us. This is a particular problem for the Sidekick. They keep giving and giving in their relationships, focused on the "passing" glory, because they don't believe they are worthy of receiving. When you get stuck in your own dark woods, think of Eyeore and be prepared to be surprised. There just might be a Hail Mary pass headed your way. ♥

Flutie's 'Hail Mary' shocks Hurricanes, by Bruce Lowitt © St. Petersburg Times, published October 20, 1999.

**A.A. Milne, *The World of Pooh: The Complete Winnie-the-Pooh* and *The House At Pooh Corner*. (New York, NY: Dutton Children's Books, 1985) 70.

Chapter Nine

Custodian

Have you ever heard that old Country Western song that goes, "Looking for love in all the wrong places, looking for love in too many faces..."?[23] Those tangles we've been talking about are "all the wrong places" to find love. But they are big and showy, aren't they? They know exactly how to get our attention and convince us that if we follow their lead, we are for sure on the path to true love.

Getting caught in those tangles is like getting fooled by a circus barker who promises us some marvelously grotesque half-human, half-orangutan, half-guinea pig for fifty cents, and all that's inside the tent is a guy wearing a monkey mask munching on wilted lettuce.

In a way, the tangles have a barker, too. Mostly the culture itself does the barking, promising us excitement, romance, and a life of wild and crazy love-making with our ideal mate if we just walk inside the BFF tent or take a chance on the Celebrity Chef's techniques. Most of the time we fall for it because we don't have a clear idea of what love is all about, so we honestly expect to find it in the most ridiculous places.

But not the Custodian. The Custodian doesn't fall for the barker's tricks, not one bit. He uses his thinking brain to counter his curiosity, no matter how many folks he sees walking inside that tent. The Custodian does not get fooled by showmanship. And so you may notice him, standing quietly next to the barker,

---

[23] Johnny Lee Ham, *Looking for Love*, 1980.

kind of smiling at you as you fork over your fifty cents, but it doesn't occur to you to ask him why he isn't going inside. If you did ask, it might save you more than spare change.

The Custodian knows what love is and where to look for it, and the most important thing a Custodian knows is that love is not an emotion. Emotions come and go; they are as changeable as the seasons and as undependable as desire. Remember the triangle? Desire does not arise from within us but is borrowed from somewhere outside of us. Our emotions ride our desires like a passenger on a roller coaster, swooping and hollering with rushes of excitement that end abruptly when the ride is over. No, real love may begin with a borrowed desire, but it will not last without our thinking brain entering into the process. What I'm getting at is that love is more than an emotion. Love is a decision.

Not very exciting, right? I mean, would you enter a circus tent where the barker was waving his hands wildly and saying, "That's right, ladies and gentlemen, step right up and see the eighth wonder of the world – two people making a decision"? Most of us wouldn't, at least not when we're young and trying to figure things out. We tend to head for the land of wild rides, big promises and happy endings – until we realize that the promises are empty and happy endings belong to fairy tales. At this point, some people decide that love makes you miserable instead of happy and is not worth all the effort. They shut their hearts to protect themselves from all the hurt. But what has hurt them is not love itself but the trap of billiard ball thinking. They've fallen into one of the tangles, and for all their struggling, they can't find a way out.

Maybe the Custodians have a way to untie the knots. Here are two comments from those who took the questionnaire. They give you an idea of how thoughtful Custodians are. They are not afraid to use their thinking brains, even if it means they'll discover some areas for self-improvement.

"True love is being able to put forth everything you own, including your time and yourself. The willingness to sacrifice your wants and needs to see the contentment of your partner! It's also about being committed and understanding, being able to accept each other's flaws, but still loving them unconditionally."

"I have been married 10 years and in the beginning I was a thrill seeker, until it almost got me a big ole divorce. I did some real soul searching and realized how selfish I was and how much my husband put in and how much I didn't. I really changed my tune, and have been married 8 more years since then. Meeting halfway, sharing, communicating and being responsive works much better!"

Custodians are not showy people. They aren't into big effects. What matters to them is finding a fulfilling, deep love that will last a lifetime. And they realize that anything that wonderful and long lasting will not just fall into their laps without effort. They will have to work for it. So when they feel a desire being aroused and an emotion starting to sweep them away, they sprinkle in a little brainpower and ask the big questions:

The BFF Question: Do I love this person because my friend loved him/her first?

The Celebrity Chef Question: Do I need my friends' approval about my choice of lover?

The Super Hero Question: Do I love this person because s/he is unattainable?

The Rock Star Question: Do I love what this person does for my image?

The Sidekick Question: Do I confuse my need to be needed with love?

I Never Wanted

This is a song for everyone who's been so wounded by the tangles of desire that they have given up on love. Despite their instinct to run away from the pain, they suspect that the only cure for their wounds is to dive back into love. "I said I never wanted love," the lyric goes, "but love is the only thing I need." Finding the courage to love again will take wisdom and strength, so here's a little theme song to hum when you need inspiration to go on.

I Never Wanted*

I never wanted to be this open
I never wanted the pain
I never wanted to feel my heart ache again
I never wanted the sacrifices
I never wanted to choose
I never wanted to play a game I might lose
But I need someone to help me feel whole
And I need someone to fill this empty soul
And I need something to give me strength to see
I said I never wanted love
But love is the only thing I need

I never wanted the aggravation
I never wanted to help
I never wanted to give so much of myself
I never wanted to say I'm sorry
I never wanted to try
I never wanted to hurt when I said goodbye

I Never Wanted, continued

But I need someone to share my life with
Oh and I need someone to heal me with their kiss
And I need something to help my heart to see
I thought I never wanted love
But love is exactly what I need

Never wanted my dreams to sit upon the shelf
Never wanted to work that hard to please somebody else
Oh no, I don't know why I never knew
It's you that I need to be someone
To tell me the truth
Oh and I need someone who's love will be the proof
And I need someone like you to make me see
I said I never wanted love
But love is the only thing I need
To love you is all I really need ❧

*John Batdorf and Michael McLean, *I Never Wanted*, 2006.

The Custodian is courageous enough to be honest about the answers, and then goes to work on applying them to his/her desires. Custodians will decide whether or not to pursue a love interest based on the answers to the big questions, plus one more. The biggest question of all:

Am I willing to work for this love?

As you might guess from the unglamorous name we've chosen for this love pattern, Custodians know that real love is hard work. It's often messy and without external rewards. They don't perform acts of love in order to be praised for being thoughtful or being the perfect lover or being a paragon of virtue. Custodians aren't in the love business for fame or recognition. They don't seek to change their lover to fit their selfish desire of what they think their lover should be like. Rather, the Custodian seeks to fulfill the desires of their lover. Their goal is not to hang onto their lover for dear life, afraid that if they don't do the right thing their lover will leave them. No, they are able to take risks in the name of love. They are willing to lose what's most important to them in order to be authentic lovers and true to themselves. One way you can tell you're dealing with a Custodian is by the way they actually take pleasure in the dirty work their lover might not like to do, including mopping the floor, washing the dishes, cleaning closets, and grocery shopping because it will make their lover happy. Their happiness comes in bringing happiness to others.

You might notice a similarity here with the Sidekick who seems as generous and giving as the Custodian. Though the Custodian knows that love requires a certain degree of vulnerability, unlike the Sidekick, the Custodian knows when to draw the line. If they find someone who abuses their love without regret, Custodians wish them well and move on.

The trick is to learn the difference, just as Marge Simpson[24] has. Her Homer is not the brightest bulb in the pack, but his heart is definitely in the right place – most of the time.

Once, on Marge's birthday, Homer gave her the gift he wanted to receive himself, a bowling ball engraved with his name. Now Marge is hurt by this – she wouldn't be human if she wasn't. (I know she's a cartoon character, but this show is funny because it's so spot on we forget.) Using the bowling ball to spite Homer, she gets her head turned by a smooth-talking Frenchman in the next lane. She goes on a few dates with him, leaving Homer home to take care of the kids and wonder if she's cheating on him. At this point, both Homer and Marge are guilty of mistakes that are hurtful to the other. But the writers know what their characters need to do to avoid going down the path of escalating resentment and get-even salvos. Instead of going for a romantic tryst with Frenchie, Marge takes a detour to Homer's work. When she arrives, instead of asking her to explain herself, Homer sweeps her off her feet and tells his co-workers, "I'll be back in ten minutes!"

With the wisdom of the Custodian, Marge used her thinking brain, and Homer found the strength to forgive instead of accuse. They understand that no one is perfect. In any relationship, mistakes will always be made, and feelings will always get hurt; but like the best BFF, they forgive because they know they need to be forgiven as well.

Forgiveness takes courage. When someone hurts you, your instinct is to hurt them back. We can explain it in terms of the desire triangle. Remember how two friends can fuel each other's desire for a particular person? It's because their talent for becoming is absorbing the desire being modeled for them and claiming it for itself. The talent for becoming cannot invent something to claim; it can only grasp after something that exists in plain sight.

---

[24] *The Simpsons*, Fox, 18 March, 1990.

That's how we get caught in those awful, endlessly painful feuds with our beloved. We are simply absorbing their desire to hurt us, making it our own and dishing it back to them with a little extra fury. Ratcheting up the conflict is what passes for originality in these situations.

It's like that movie with Michael Douglas and Kathleen Turner, *War of the Roses*.[25] They play a couple going through a divorce, but neither wants to vacate their expensive house because if they do, the other one will get it in the settlement. So they launch a campaign to get the other to leave. Their antics grow more vicious and ridiculous as the movie goes on. What's really interesting is that the most original and independent thing either one of them could do would be to forgive, to surrender, to say, "Okay, you win! Take the darn house, if it's that important to you." That would take courage and the strength of character to "lose" the battle for the house. But can there really be a winner in such a vindictive struggle? When love turns to hate, the victor is the one who was most willing to abandon all decency and self-respect to defeat their lover/rival. To win such a battle is to lose your soul. To forgive is to open up the possibility of recovering the love that has been ravaged in a match for the title of most ruthless, heartless, vindictive ex-spouse who ever played the divorce game.

To forgive, to be willing to lose such battles, will put you on the Custodian's path to true love. You will know you are on the right road when your relationships show signs of commitment, contentment, and abiding joy. Where others seek the drama of conflict, Custodians seek shared pleasure. Where others need thrills, Custodians thrill in discovering their beloved's soul.

[25] *War of the Roses*, dir. Danny DeVito, writs. Warren Adler and Michael Leeson, perfs. Michael Douglas, Kathleen Turner and Danny DeVito, DVD, Gracie Films, 1989.

Custodian

Where others grasp desperately to acquire love, Custodians find that, paradoxically, the more they give, the more their needs are satisfied.

It's the unconventional truth that when we are seeking to possess a lover, love will forever slip through our fingers. But when we seek to give rather than get, to love rather than be loved, we will find the road to true love open up before us.

Never Had to Ask

When it happens, it feels like a miracle. How else to explain that love shows up when you aren't looking for it, that it offers itself when you've given up asking for it? Let this song become your new love melody for it expresses the truth too often hidden by romantic ballads about "winning" someone's heart. This is the unexpected flip side of the hard work of the Custodian, the surprising ease of discovering that there is nothing you can do to earn, deserve, win or acquire love. Sing this song to remind you of the miraculous and ever present possibility of love.

Never Had to Ask*

In the sweetest dreams I've ever known
I could barely glimpse a love like you have shown
I'm not sure I'm every gonna see
Why you've given all the love you have to me

Cause I'd have given all I have
Volunteered for any task
Just to feel a love like yours
But I never, never had to ask

You were there when everyone was gone
Led me to a loving place where I'd belong
Even though I never said a word
Was there something in my aching heart you heard

I'd have begged you all my life
On my knees on broken glass
For these moments in your light
But I never, never had to ask

Never Had to Ask, continued

It's almost like your mind can read my heart
And you're listening to my secret prayer
Even when I'm lost when we're apart
I feel your love so near

Since your love's encompassed me
I will never have to ask
If a love could, could ever last
No I'll never ever have to ask
Never have to ask ❤

*John Batdorf/Michael McLean, *Never Had To Ask*, 1997.

Chapter Ten

Love is An Eternal Mystery...
and Gift.

'd like to end with a few last thoughts about what love is. We've been dealing with the image of getting all caught up in the messy rope of tangled desires. The best way to free ourselves from that tangled cord is to think of love as a gift with no strings attached. In fact, love is not just *a* gift, it is Gift itself.[26]

What does that mean? Well, *a* gift is too often something we give one another that somehow or other seems to tie us into an obligation to give something back. Think of people with whom you exchange birthday presents. It's always someone who gives *you* a gift on *your* birthday. If someone outside of that circle happens to give you a gift, don't you feel obligated to find out when their birthday is and return the giving?

Or what happens when the person you gave a $15 wall plaque that says, "You can pick your friends, you can pick your nose, but you can't pick your friend's nose," gives you a pair of tickets to a concert worth $150? Don't you feel embarrassed and in debt to them? The expensive gift feels like one-upmanship, with you on the bottom and your friend on top. You can't wait till his birthday comes to turn the tables by giving him a $200 cash-

---

[26] For the analysis of love and relationship in this chapter, I am indebted to the third chapter of *À charge de revanche: Figures élémentaires de la réciprocité* by Mark Rogin Anspach (Paris: Éditions du Seuil, 2002). Translation by Anspach.

mere sweater with his initials monogrammed on it. Because a gift almost always involves a reciprocal obligation that turns into a game of "Can you top this?" It becomes all about making sure your gift earns you more prestige points than your friend's gift earned him.

Okay, that is NOT what love is. Love is Gift – giving without any expectation of getting something in return. It is simply the giving itself with no strings attached. When you give that way, you form a different type of relationship with the person you are giving to. With *a* gift, it's too often a competitive relationship disguised as generosity that creates tensions and resentments. To avoid this, friends and family will often put a spending limit on gifts or decide together that the gifts must all be homemade. Better yet, some friends and family dispense with gift giving altogether and just spend time together. That at least avoids the risk that someone will get caught up in the game of competitive gift giving.

Love is giving non-competitively. When two people engage in this kind of giving, something remarkable happens. They begin to build something new that did not exist before. Often we call this thing the "relationship," though it's different than the competitive relationships we usually have. The love relationship is bigger than the sum of the parts, as the saying goes. When you find someone whom you decide to love, you will be giving the gift of yourself to them with no strings attached, and they will be giving the gift of themselves to you with no strings attached *for the rest of your lives*. (That part is important.) You begin to build a "relationship" which is the two of you, but is also more than the two of you. I like to think of it as constructing a safe place where you can just be, and no one is going to judge you or hold anything against you or keep tabs on who has been giving more or less than the other person.

Now this kind of thing requires a great deal of trust, which is why you can't enter into it thinking that it has the shelf life of ripe avocados. No, this thing you are entering into together better last longer than Twinkies® or there's no way you'd be that open, that vulnerable, that giving with someone. Love is making yourself as open to another human being as you can be, and if you can't trust that they will love you no matter what they see behind your carefully groomed facade, then the experiment is doomed to failure. The high spin, high maintenance "relationship" will be a sham.

The only way it can work is if both of you decide that the "relationship" is more valuable than any earthly treasure you can imagine, even greater than any earthly treasure you possess, which you are willingly giving to your lover anyway with no strings attached (that means no pre-nups). It is even worth more to you than finding relief from the hard work and pain of self-discovery that being in a relationship inflicts on you from time to time.

That's why the Custodian gets it. The Custodian is not afraid of hard work, getting dirty, or appearing to be a fool by the standards of the world. Marge Simpson is a great example of this. She doesn't care if no one else appreciates how great Homer is. In fact, everyone thinks she's crazy to be with him. She's definitely not in the business of loving Homer to enhance her reputation. Her love for Homer demonstrates that there are no ego needs to be served when love is Gift; there can't be. Ego is all about self-preservation, and love is about giving yourself away, so they just don't go together at all.

You may have noticed as you were reading about the tangles of desire that they all have to do with taking care of yourself – protecting your image, enhancing your reputation or possessing a lover. Behind all the tangles is this idea that love is something you can acquire, a kind of ego-inflating prize you can win if you play the love game well enough. But that's as much of a dead end as competitive gift giving. Competitive love is an endless round of disappointment which can lead you to give up on finding love altogether.

So we are faced with a paradox: Love cannot be acquired; it can only be given and received. The wicked truth about love is that the more you are able to give it to someone with no strings attached, the more you will find yourself surrounded by true love. Isn't that mysterious?

How do you get to that place where you can give love without expecting anything in return? There is no quick and easy answer to that one, but a good place to begin is to ask yourself those big questions from the last chapter so that you can be sure that your talent for becoming and your thinking brain are *both* involved in your love relationships. Then you have to learn how to tell the difference between the hard work and occasional pain of true love and the abuse of the Sidekick tangle. It's sad but true that some people can only be loved from a distance. When you encounter those people, you need to be strong enough to disentangle yourself from them without becoming consumed with hard feelings or the desire to get even. Just wish them well and move on.

So now you know the truth about desire, and you can see through all the tangles that might trip you up on the way to true love. Here's one last thing to remember before you close this book and recommit yourself to the task of building a lasting love relationship: when you free yourself from all the borrowed desires that have led you astray, you are not going to find hidden deep inside yourself some real, true authentic desire. What you will find is that during that process of peeling away others' desires, you will begin to realize that you are completely loveable just the way you are without needing to acquire or achieve or possess one more thing. You will discover an inner contentment that allows you to relate to others in a completely new way. Instead of trying to possess them or change them or use them for your own purposes, your vision will clear, and you will see NOT what they can do for you, but who they truly are. You will realize that you don't need them – you *treasure* them. It is when you don't need anyone or anything at all that you will become able to give and receive the Gift that is love.

Celebrate the mystery. Be the Gift.